DIDCOT TO WINCHESTER

Vic Mitchell and Keith Smith

MP Middleton Press

First published May 1998
First reprint March 2006
Second reprint October 2010

ISBN 978 1 901706 13 0

© Middleton Press, 1998

Design   Deborah Esher
Typesetting   Barbara Mitchell

Published by
          Middleton Press
          Easebourne Lane
          Midhurst, West Sussex
          GU29 9AZ
Tel: 01730 813169
Fax: 01730 812601
Email: info@middletonpress.co.uk
www..middletonpress.co.uk

Printed in the United Kingdom by Henry Ling Limited, at the Dorset Press, Dorchester, DT1 1HD

INDEX

ACKNOWLEDGEMENTS

We are sincerely grateful for the help received from N.Langridge, Mrs B.Mitchell, Ms L.Rutter, Mr D. & Dr S. Salter, R.Simmonds and E.Youldon.

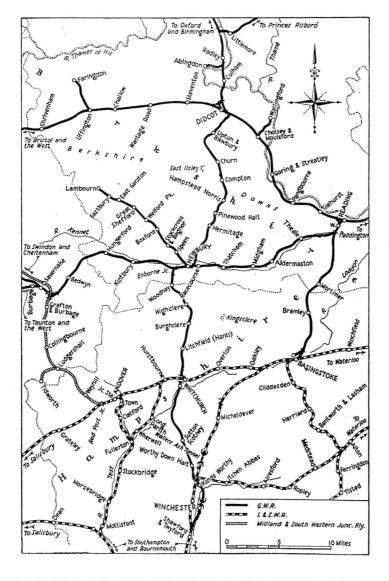

Railways of the area in 1922. (Railway Magazine)

GEOGRAPHICAL SETTING

The first four miles from Didcot involves climbing away from the Thames Valley onto the chalk uplands on which the line remains until descending into the Kennet Valley at Newbury. The geology is almost entirely Chalk, with some overlying Clay in the vicinity of Hermitage and Alluvium with Gravels in the valleys.

High chalkland is regained after another climb and similar geology prevails all the way to Winchester. The River Test is crossed at Whitchurch and one of its tributaries is bridged at Sutton Scotney. The Itchen Valley is followed from Kings Worthy to Shawford Junction, through the ancient city of Winchester, once capital of England.

Maps herein are to the scale of 25 ins to 1 mile. North is at the top in each case and they are from the 1910 edition, unless otherwise indicated.

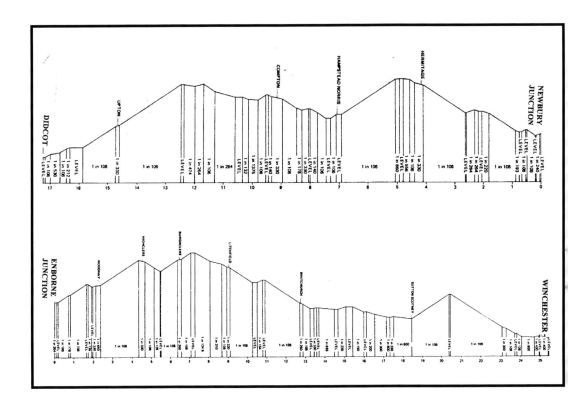

HISTORICAL BACKGROUND

The Great Western Railway's lines from London reached Didcot in 1840 and Newbury in 1847. The London & South Western Railway's routes from the capital were opened to Winchester in 1840 and to Whitchurch in 1854.

It was onto this network of radiating lines that the Didcot, Newbury & Southampton Railway was projected. The company received its Act for construction on 5th August 1873 and provision was made in the structures for double track.

The Didcot-Newbury section came into use on 13th April 1882, followed by the Newbury-

Winchester part on 1st May 1885. Financial difficulties meant that the planned independent route to Southampton could not be completed, although a viaduct was started in that town. The company had to accept the frustrations of using the LSWR tracks in this area, after the Winchester-Shawford Junction section eventually opened on 1st October 1891.

The entire route was operated by the GWR, although LSWR locomotives hauled most trains south of Winchester until 1910. The DNSR was absorbed by the GWR in 1923, but it continued to show little interest in the line. It preferred to send its heavy north-south freight traffic by less steeply graded routes, but during World War II these were congested on many occasions. Thus it was decided to double much of the DNS and the line was closed as a through route during the daytime from 4th August 1942 to 8th March 1943, to speed the process. It became an essential link between the armament and military equipment suppliers of the Midlands and the South Coast ports before and after the invasion of Europe.

Prior to D-Day, 16000 military trains were operated over the line.

The Railway Magazine proudly announced in November 1944 that notable alterations had taken place on a GWR line "which cannot be identified for security reasons. All the existing loops have been extended from 300 to 550 yds and three extra loops have been laid. A mile-long connection to another company has been laid at the southern end, to improve traffic flow, and the northern 20 miles have been doubled" (i.e. to Woodhay).

Upon nationalisation in 1948, the line became part of the Western Region of British Railways but the section south of Newbury was transferred to the Southern Region on 2nd April 1950. This part was closed to passengers on 7th March 1960 and the northern section followed on 10th September 1962.

Through freight traffic continued until 9th August 1964; local withdrawal dates are given in the captions, as are details of a temporary passenger revival at Winchester Chesil (caption 119).

PASSENGER SERVICES

There were four or five stopping trains each way weekdays only for most of the life of the line, with six south of Newbury for many years. One Sunday train was provided from 1927 to 1933 but, on the northern half only, between 1934 and 1946, milk conveyance being the main reason for these services.

A fast train in the down direction was tried briefly in 1895. Through coaches between Leicester and Southampton via the Great Central Railway were introduced in 1901 and a restaurant train to Newcastle commenced in 1903. A through

service between Paddington and Southampton via Newbury started in 1898 but this was changed in 1901 to a slip coach off a down Weymouth Express. These developments ceased with the advent of World War I. A through coach from Paddington ran again in 1922-23 and through coaches to Edinburgh ran between 1922 and 1939, in the up direction only.

During most of the 1930s and 40s, a late evening train ran north from Winchester, mainly to serve the many military camps. Four trains each way sufficed from mid-Summer of 1958.

September 1885

July 1882

DIDCOT and NEWBURY.—Great Western.

DIDCOT, NEWBURY, and WINCHESTER.—Great Western.

DIDCOT, NEWBURY, WINCHESTER, and SOUTHAMPTON.—Didcot, Newbury, and Southampton.

Down.	mrn	mrn	mrn	mrn	aft	aft	aft	aft	aft	aft	
Didcot ....dep.	c Leaves at 9 7 mrn., changing at Eastleigh.	7 45	....	1033	1250	....	2 57	....	6 32	Satrdys only.	....
Upton		7 55	....	1041	....	....	3 5	....	6 40		....
Compton		8 9	....	1056	1 6	....	3 18	....	6 53		....
Hampstead Norris..		8 14	....	11 1	d	....	3 23	....	6 58		....
Hermitage		8 23	....	11 9	1 19	....	3 31	....	7 6		....
Newbury 20, 21 arr.		8 33	....	1117	1 27	....	3 39	....	7 14		....
2 London (Pad.) dep.		6 30	....	9 5	12 0	....	1 45	5 45	5 45	7 0	....
Newbury ....dep.		8 55	....	1130	1 40	....	3 55	7 0	7 20	9 45	....
Woodhay		9 5	....	1140	1 49	....	4 4	a	7 29	9 54	....
Highclere		9 14	....	1149	....	....	4 12	....	7 37	10 3	....
Burghclere...........		9 20	....	1156	1 59	....	4 17	a	7 42	10 9	....
Litchfield ....[84		9 27	....	12 3	....	....	4 23	a	7 48	1016	....
Whitchurch 86, 88,		9 38	....	1212	2 10	....	4 30	a	7 55	1024	....
Sutton Scotney......		9 52	....	1228	2 21	....	4 41	a	8 6	1035	....
Winchester * 76, 96 arr.		10 4	....	1240	2 33	....	4 53	7 48	8 17	1047	....
Winchester * 76, 96 dep.	9 10	10 8	....	1245	2 43	....	4 57	7 52	8 19	1129	b
Shawford & Twyford	9 18	1016	....	1253	2 51	....	5 5	....	8 27	....	....
Eastleigh † 82, 86 ..	9 24	1022	1035	1258	2 57	3 6	5 12	8 5	8 33	1139	....
Swaythling	9 30	⌐	1045	1 5	⌐	3 11	5 18	....	8 40	....	....
St. Denys............	9 34	....	1052	1 9	....	3 15	5 22	8 13	8 44	....	....
Northam	9 36	1032	....	1 12	3 6	3 18	5 25	8 16	8 47	1153	....
Southampton ‡ arr.	9 40	1037	....	1 17	3 11	3 23	5 29	8 20	8 52	12 0	....

Up.	Fares from Southamptn 1 cl. s. d.	2 cl. s. d.	3 cl. s. d.	mrn	mrn	mrn	mrn	mrn	mrn	mrn	aft	aft	aft
Southampton ..dep.				6 50	7 8	8 20	9 8	1050	1133	1142	2 10	5 30	7 55
Northam				6 54	....	8 23	9 11	1054	1136	....	2 14	5 33	7 59
St. Denys				6 58	7 13	8 27	9 15	1058	1141	1147	2 18	5 36	8 2
Swaythling.........	....	....	....	7 2	....	8 31	e	11 2	1145	....	....	....	8 6
Eastleigh †..........	....	....	....	7 7	7 21	8 37	9 22	11 9	1150	1156	2 25	5 44	8 13
Shawford & Twyford	....	....	....	⌐	....	8 46	d	1119	⌐	c	2 34	5 53	8 23
Winchester * 79, 96 arr.	2 0	1 3	1 0	....	7 33	8 55	9 35	1127	....	12 8	2 41	6 0	8 29
Winchester * 79, 96 dep.				....	7 38	9 15	9 40	‡ Town and Dock Station.	....	1213	2 46	6 5	8 34
Sutton Scotney......	3 2	2 0	1 7	....	7 51	9 28	9 52		....	1226	2 59	6 18	8 47
Whitchurch..........	4 0	2 7	2 0½	....	8 1	9 38	d		....	1236	3 10	6 28	8 57
Litchfield	4 8	2 11	2 4	....	8 10	9 47	....		....	1245	3 19	6 37	9 6
Burghclere...........	5 2	3 3	2 7	....	8 16	9 53	d		....	1251	3 25	6 43	9 12
Highclere	5 6	3 6	2 9	....	8 21	9 58	....		....	1256	3 30	6 48	9 17
Woodhay	5 10	3 9	2 11	....	8 27	10 4	....		....	1 2	3 36	6 54	9 23
Newbury 20, 21 arr.	6 6	4 1	3 2½	....	8 35	1013	1027		....	1 10	3 45	7 2	9 32
11 London (Pad.) arr.	13 0	8 2	6 6	....	1010	1145	1145		....	2 50	5 50	9 10	1140
Newbury ....dep.	....	....	....	....	9 5	....	1033		....	1 26	3 53	7 15	Satrdys only.
Hermitage	7 2	4 6	3 7	....	9 14	....	1042		....	1 35	4 3	7 25	
Hampstead Norris..	7 8	4 9	3 10	....	9 21	....	1049		....	1 42	4 11	7 33	
Compton	8 0	5 0	4 0	....	9 28	....	1055		....	1 50	4 17	7 39	
Upton	9 0	5 7	4 5½	....	9 40	....	11 7		....	2 1	4 29	7 51	
Didcot 34, 10, 2 arr.	9 6	5 11	4 8½	....	9 46	....	1113		....	2 7	4 37	7 57	

a Stops when required to set down from London. **b** Departs from L. & S. W. Station. **c** Stops when required to take up for Newbury and beyond. **d** Stop when required to take up for Paddington. * Cheesehill Street; one mile from the L. & S. W. Station. † Eastleigh and Bishopstoke.

December 1895

DIDCOT, NEWBURY, WINCHESTER, and SOUTHAMPTON.—
Didcot, Newbury, and Southampton.

July 1899

Down.	mrn	mrn	aft	aft	aft	aft
Didcot ....dep.	7 45	1035	1245	1 30	6 25	Satrdys. only.
Upton	7 55	1042	....	1 38	6 33	
Compton	8 9	1058	1 1	1 54	6 46	
Hampstead Norris..	8 14	11 8	....	1 59	6 51	
Hermitage	8 23	1111	1 11	2 7	6 59	
Newbury 14 arr.	8 33	1119	1 19	2 15	7 8	
Newbury 14 dep.	8 58	1125	1 20	2 25	7 10	9 45
Woodhay	9 7	1134	1 32	2 34	7 19	9 54
Highclere..........	9 16	1143	....	2 43	7 28	10 3
Burghclere	9 22	1149	....	2 49	7 34	10 9
Litchfield ......[76	9 28	1156	....	2 58	7 41	10 16
Whitchurch 70, 72,	9 37	12 4	1 52	3 9	7 49	10 24
Sutton Scotney	9 49	1215	2 3	3 20	8 0	10 35
Winchester * 64, 80 arr.	10 1	1227	2 15	3 33	8 13	10 48
Winchester * 64, 80 dep.	10 5	1233	2 20	3 38	8 18	11b29
Shawford †	1013	1242	....	3 47	8 27	....
Eastleigh ‡ 63, 70..	1019	1250	2 35	3 54	8 35	11 46
Swaythling	....	1255	....	3 59	8 40	....
St. Denys	....	1259	....	4 3	8 44	....
Northam...........	1028	1 4	2 45	4 8	8 49	11 56
Southampton arr.	1031	1 7	2 48	4 10	8 52	11 58

Up.	mrn	mrn	mrn	mrn	mrn	mrn	mrn	aft	aft	aft
Southampton.	6 50	7 8	8 55	9 8	1050	1133	1150	2 10	5 35	7 55
Northam	6 54	....	8 59	....	1054	1136	....	2 14	5 38	7 59
St. Denys......	6 58	7 13	9 3	....	1058	1139	....	2 18	5 41	8 3
Swaythling ...	7 2	....	9 7	....	11 2	1143	....	....	....	8 7
Eastleigh ‡.....	7 7	7 20	9 12	9 18	11 9	1148	12 5	2 25	5 49	8 13
Shawford †.....	⌐	....	⌐	Sat.	1118	⌐	....	2 34	5 57	8 22
Winchester * 66, 80 arr.		7 35	† Shawford and Twyford. ‡ Eastleigh & Bishopstoke.	9 32	1126	* Cheesehill Street; one mile from the L. & S. W. Station.	1220	2 42	6 5	8 28
Winchester * 66, 80 dep.		7 40		9 36	b Departs from L. & S. W. Station.		1228	2 46	6 10	8 30
Sutton Scotney		7 54		9 49			1241	2 59	6 24	8 44
Whitchurch		8 5		9 59			1252	3 10	6 35	8 55
Litchfield.........		8 14		10 8			1 1	3 19	6 41	9 4
Burghclere		8 20		1014			1 8	3 25	6 50	9 10
Highclere		8 25		1019			1 13	3 30	6 55	9 15
Woodhay		8 31		1025			1 20	3 36	7 1	9 21
Newbury 14 arr.		8 40		1033			1 29	3 45	7 10	9 30
Newbury 14 dep.		9 20		1035			1 31	3 53	7 13	Satrdys. only.
Hermitage		9 30		1044			1 40	4 3	7 23	
Hampstead Norris..		9 38		1051			1 47	4 11	7 31	
Compton		9 44		1058			1 54	4 17	7 37	
Upton		9 56		1110			2 6	4 29	7 49	
Didcot 30, 8, 2 arr.		10 2		1116			2 12	4 37	7 55	

January 1934

DIDCOT, NEWBURY, WINCHESTER, and SOUTHAMPTON TERMINUS.

Miles.	Down.	Week Days. mrn	mrn	mrn	mrn		aft	aft	aft	aft	Suns. aft	
	36 London (Pad.)...dep.	..	5 30	8 40	11A15	..	1 45	3 35	5 15	Saturdays only.	1245	..
	103 Oxford .... "	..	7 10	9 50	11 35	..	2 50	4 58	6 5		1 0	..
—	Didcot.............dep.	..	7 38	1020	12 35	..	3 35	5 52	6 47		3 0	..
3	Upton and Blewbury....	..	7 46	1030	12 42	..	3 43	5 59	6 54		3 8	..
6¼	Churn	..	7 53	Aa	Aa	..	Aa	Aa	Aa		..	..
8¼	Compton	..	7 58	1042	12 56	..	3 55	6 13	7 7		3 21	..
10½	Hampstead Norris.......	..	8 3	1047	1 1	..	4 0	6 19	7 12		3 27	..
12¼	Pinewood Halt...........	..	8 9	1053	1 7	..	4 6	6 25	7 18		3 33	..
13½	Hermitage	..	8 14	1056	1 10	..	4 10	6 28	7 23		3 36	..
18	Newbury 2, 8, 54...arr.	..	8 23	11 5	1 19	..	4 18	6 37	7 35		3 45	..
—	2 London (Pad.)...dep.	..	7 15	1045	12 30	..	2 45	6 0	..	7 55	..	..
—	Newbury ....dep.	7 45	9 5	1225	2 0	..	4 28	7 18	..	1020	..	..
21¼	Woodhay	7 53	9 16	1233	2 7	..	4 37	7 26	..	1028	..	..
23¼	Highclere	8 5	9 22	1238	2 13	..	4 43	7 32	..	1034	..	..
25½	Burghclere A	8 10	9 27	1243	2 18	..	4 48	7 37	..	1039	..	..
28	Litchfield (Hants.).......	8 16	9 33	1248	2 23	..	4 54	7 43	..	1045	..	..
31¼	Whitchurch B 176......	8 23	9 40	1255	2 30	..	5 1	7 50	..	1052	..	..
37¼	Sutton Scotney..........	8 36	9 50	1 4	2 39	..	5 11	8 0	..	11 2	..	..
40¼	Worthy Down Platform.	8 42	9 56	1 10	2 45	..	5 17	8 6	..	..	..	..
42½	King's Worthy	8 47	10 1	1 15	2 52	..	5 22	8 11	..	1112	..	..
44½	Winchester C..... arr.	8 51	10 5	1 19	2 56	..	5 26	8 15	..	1116	..	..
	Winchester C..... dep.	8 58	1014	1 22	3 2	..	5 31	8 25	..	..	..	..
47½	Shawford D 159.........	9 5	1021	1 29	3 9	..	5 38	8 32	..	..	..	..
51½	Eastleigh F 184, 190...	9 13	1027	1 36	3 16	..	5 45	8 39	..	..	..	..
53¼	Swaythling...............	9 20	1034	28 1	3 22	..	5 56	8 47	..	..	..	..
55	St. Denys................	9 24	1038	28 5	3 26	..	6 0	8 51	..	..	..	..
56	Northam.................	9 28	1042	2810	3 30	..	6 4	8 55	..	..	..	..
56½	SouthamptonTer. G arr.	9 32	1046	2814	3 34	..	6 8	8 59	..	..	..	..

Miles	Up.	Week Days. mrn	mrn	K	mrn	mrn	aft	aft	aft	aft	aft		Suns. aft	
	Southampton Ter. .dep.	..	..	7J33	9 40	1130	2 5	4 52	..	7 30	Sats. only.	..	..	..
¾	Northam	..	..	7 36	9 43	1133	2 8	4 55	..	7 33		..	..	..
1¼	St. Denys...............	..	..	7 40	9 47	1137	2 12	4 59	..	7 37		..	..	..
3¼	Swaythling	..	..	7 44	9 51	1141	2 16	5 3	..	7 41		..	..	..
5½	Eastleigh F.............	..	..	7 51	9 58	1148	2 22	5 10	..	7 48		..	..	..
9½	Shawford D.............	..	..	8 0	10 5	1156	2 34	5 18	..	7 56		..	..	..
12½	Winchester C.... arr.	..	..	8 8	1013	12 4	2 41	5 26	..	8 4		..	..	..
	Winchester C.... dep	..	7 5	8 16	1023	1210	2 46	5 33	..	⌐	8 50	..	..	..
14¼	King's Worthy..........	..	7 14	8 22	1029	1216	2 52	5 39	..	..	8 56	..	..	..
16¼	Worthy Down Platform	..	7 19	8 27	1034	1221	2 57	5 44	..	..	Bb	..	..	..
19¼	Sutton Scotney.........	..	7 27	8 35	1042	1228	3 3	5 51	..	..	9 8	..	..	..
25	Whitchurch B 176	..	7 37	8 45	1052	1239	3 13	6 1	..	..	9 18	..	..	..
28¾	Litchfield (Hants).......	..	7 47	8 53	11 1	1250	3 20	6 9	..	..	9 26	..	..	..
31¼	Burghclere A...........	..	7 57	9 0	11 8	1256	3 26	6 15	..	..	9 32	..	..	..
33¾	Highclere...............	..	8 4	9 7	1113	1 1	3 31	6 20	..	..	9 37	..	..	..
35¾	Woodhay...............	..	8 15	9 15	1118	1 6	3 36	6 25	..	..	9 42	..	..	..
38¼	Newbury 2, 8, 54..arr.	..	8 22	9 22	1128	1 15	3 48	6 32	..	..	9 50	..	..	..
91¼	8 London (Pad.) ..arr.	..	10 0	1050	1255	2 55	5 50	8 10	..	..	..	..	..	..
—	Newbury...........dep.	6 45	8 28	9 28	..	1 45	4 0	7 11	8 10	..	1020	..	7 58	..
43¼	Hermitage..............	6 55	8 38	9 37	..	1 54	4 11	7 21	8 19	..	1029	..	8 8	..
44	Pinewood Halt..........	6 58	..	..	..	1 57	4 14	7 24	8 22	..	1032	..	8 11	..
46¼	Hampstead Norris......	7 5	8 46	9 44	..	2 4	4 21	7 31	8 29	..	1039	..	8 18	..
48¼	Compton................	7 10	8 53	9 50	..	2 10	4 27	7 36	8 35	..	1045	..	8 26	..
50	Churn	..	Kk	Kk	..	Kk	Kk	Kk	Kk	..	..	..	..	..
53¼	Upton and Blewbury ...	7 20	9 3	10 0	..	2 20	4 39	7 47	8 45	..	1055	..	8 37	..
56¼	Didcot 14, 40, 98..arr.	7 26	9 10	10 6	..	2 26	4 48	7 53	8 51	..	11 1	..	8 43	..
67	98 Oxford........arr.	8 35	10 9	1037	..	3 22	5 25	8 30	9 16	..	1130	..	9 39	..
110	40 London (Pad.).. "	9 0	1015	1155	..	5 22	6 15	..	10 25	..	2 40	..	10 0	..

A Station for Kingsclere (3¼ miles).
A By Slip Carriage.
Aa Stops when required to take up or to set down on previous notice being given to the Station Master at Didcot. Evening trains call during daylight only.
B Hants; about 1¼ mls. to Southern Sta.
8 Change at Eastleigh.
Bb Stops to set down on informing the Guard at Winchester.
C Cheesehill; 1 mile from Southern Sta.
D Station for Twyford.
F Station for Bishopstoke.
G Station for Docks.
J Starts from **Southampton Docks** at 7 5 mrn. on Weds. and Fris. in connection with Steamer from Havre.
K Restaurant Car, Oxford to Newcastle. Thro' Carriages to Edinburgh (W.), and Glasgow (Q. St.), pages 99, 844, 704, 824, and 9.0.
Kk Stops to take up or set down on giving notice to Station Master at Newbury. Evening trains call during daylight only.

DIDCOT, NEWBURY, WINCHESTER, and SOUTHAMPTON TERMINUS

Miles	Down	Week Days mrn	mrn	mrn	aft	mrn	aft	aft	aft		Suns. aft	
	36London (Pad.)..... dep	..	5 30	S	S	10N3	1 45	3 15	4 45	..	1230	..
	103Oxford .... "	..	7N10	..	..	10N55	3 0	4N55	5 50	..	1 55	..
—	Didcot.............. dep	..	7 37	..	..	12 45	3 35	5 52	6 30	..	3 0	..
3	Upton and Blewbury....	..	7 45	..	..	12 52	3 42	5 59	..	..	3 8	..
6¾	Churn	..	7 52	..	..	Aa	Aa	Aa	..	..	..	..
8½	Compton	..	7 58	..	..	1 6	3 54	6 11	..	..	3 21	..
10½	Hampstead Norris.......	..	8 3	..	..	1 11	3 59	6 17	..	..	3 27	..
12¾	Pinewood Halt..........	..	8 9	..	..	1 17	4 5	6 24	..	..	3 33	..
13½	Hermitage..............	..	8 15	..	..	1 22	4 10	6 29	..	..	3 37	..
18	**Newbury 1, 8, 54... arr**	..	8 25	..	..	1 30	4 18	6 38	7 20	..	3 45	..
—	1 London (Pad.).... dep	..	6 20	8 55	..	12 30	1 55	6 0	..	..	..	..
—	**Newbury**........... dep	7 45	9 5	1235	..	2 0	4 25	7 18		..	..	..
21½	Woodhay	7 53	9 16	1242	..	2 10	4 33	7 28		..	..	..
23½	Highclere..............	8 2	9 22	1248	..	2 16	4 39	7 36		..	..	..
25½	Burghclere **A**...........	8 8	9 27	1255	..	2 21	4 44	7 41		..	..	..
28	Litchfield (Hants.)......	8 15	9 33	1 2	③	2 27	4 50	7 47		..	..	..
31¾	Whitchurch (Hants.) 170	8 22	9 40	1 8	1 40	2 34	4 57	7 55	Limited accommodation Third class only	..	..	..
37½	Sutton Scotney..........	8 35	9 50	③	1 50	2 44	5 7	8 6		..	..	..
40¼	Worthy Down Platform	8 42	9 56	..	..	2 50	5 13	8 12		..	..	..
42½	King's Worthy..........	8 47	10 2	..	2 0	2 56	5 19	8 18		..	..	..
44½	**Winchester C**.... arr	8 51	10 6	..	2 5	3 0	5 23	8 22		..	..	..
	dep	9 6	1014	..	..	3 5	5 38	8 28		..	..	..
47½	Shawford **D** 159	9 13	1021	..	..	3 14	5 47	8 37		..	..	..
51½	Eastleigh **F** 184, 187....	9 21	1028	..	..	3 22	5 54	8 44		..	..	..
53½	Swaythling	..	1036	..	..	3B40	6 1	8 51		..	..	..
55	St. Denys...............	9 29	1040	..	..	3B44	6 5	8 55		..	..	..
56	Northam	..	1043	..	..	3B48	6 9	8 59		..	..	..
56¾	Southampton Ter. **G** arr	9 35	1047	..	..	3B52	6 13	9 3		..	..	..

Miles	Up	Week Days mrn	mrn	mrn	mrn		aft	aft	aft	aft	aft	aft	Suns. aft	
	Southampton Ter... dep	..	..	7 32	1133	..	..	2 0	4 55	..	7 35	..	..	..
½	Northam	..	..	7 35	1136	..	..	2 3	4 58	..	7 38	..	..	..
1½	St. Denys	..	..	7 39	1140	..	..	2 7	5 2	..	7 42	..	..	..
3¼	Swaythling	..	..	7 43	1144	..	..	2 11	5 5	..	7 46	..	..	..
5½	Eastleigh **F**	..	..	7 51	1156	..	..	2 20	5 12	..	7 56	..	..	..
9½	Shawford **D**............	..	..	8 0	12 3	..	..	2 29	5 19	..	8 3	..	..	..
12½	**Winchester C**.... arr	..	..	8 8	1211	..	..	2 37	5 27	..	8 11	..	..	..
	dep	..	7 5	8 14	1214	..	..	2 42	5 33	..	..	1130	..	..
14½	King's Worthy..........	..	7 10	8 20	1220	..	..	2 52	5 39	..	..	1135	..	..
16½	Worthy Down Platform	..	7 16	8 25	1225	..	..	2 57	5 44	..	..	1145	..	..
19½	Sutton Scotney..........	..	7 25	8 35	1231	..	..	3 8	5 50	..	..	1156	..	..
25	Whitchurch (Hants.) 170	..	7 40	8 45	1241	..	..	3 22	6 0	..	..	..	..	..
28½	Litchfield (Hants.)......	..	7 49	8 53	1249	..	..	3 32	6 9	..	..	..	..	..
31½	Burghclere **A**	..	7 56	9 0	1258	..	..	3 38	6 15	..	..	..	..	..
33½	Highclere..............	..	8 2	9 7	1 3	..	..	3 43	6 20	..	..	..	..	..
35½	Woodhay	..	8 10	9 15	1 8	..	..	3 48	6 25	..	..	..	..	..
38½	**Newbury 1, 8, 54... arr**	..	8 18	9 22	1 15	..	..	3 58	6 32	..	..	..	..	..
91½	8 London (Pad.).... arr	..	1015	11 15	3 15	..	..	6J40	8N30	..	..	..	..	..
—	**Newbury**........... dep	6 45	..	9 35	..	..	1 55	4 20	..	7 22	..	..	8 10	..
43½	Hermitage..............	6 55	..	9 45	..	..	2 4	4 30	..	7 32	..	..	8 20	..
44	Pinewood Halt	6 58	..	9 48	..	..	2 7	4 33	..	7 35	..	..	8 24	..
46½	Hampstead Norris.......	7 3	..	9 56	..	..	2 15	4 42	..	7 43	..	..	8 32	..
48½	Compton	7 10	..	10 3	..	..	2 20	4 50	..	7 49	..	..	8 40	..
50	Churn	..	..	Kk	..	..	Kk	Kk	..	Kk	..	..	..	..
53½	Upton and Blewbury....	7 20	..	10 14	..	..	2 32	5 0	..	8 0	..	..	8 52	..
56½	Didcot 14, 40, 98.... arr	7 28	..	10 20	..	..	2 38	5 8	..	8 10	..	..	9 0	..
67	98Oxford .... arr	9 15	..	11N12	..	..	3 25	5 45	..	9 30	..	..	9 32	..
110	40London (Pad.) ... "	9N5	..	12 5	..	..	5N37	7 25	..	9 45	..	..	1035	..

A Station for Kingsclere (3¾ miles)
Aa Stops to take up or set down on previous notice to Station Master at Didcot. Evening trains call during daylight only
B Change at Eastleigh
C Cheesehill
D Station for Twyford
F Station for Bishopstoke
G Station for Docks
J Arr. 7 8 aft on Sats. Third class only
Kk Stops to take up or set down on previous notice to Station Master at Newbury. Evening trains call during daylight only
N Third class only
S Saturdays only
③ Third class only

April 1943

November 1959

DIDCOT, NEWBURY, WINCHESTER and SOUTHAMPTON

WEEK DAYS ONLY

Miles		am	am	am		am	am		pm	pm		pm	pm		pm	pm		pm		pm	pm
	152Oxford .. .. .. dep	7 10	..	..	..	10 25	..	..	..	..	..	1 38	2 56	..	..	..	..	4 55	..	..	..
—	**Didcot**........... dep	7 40	..	..	..	10 50	..	..	..	..	..	2 5	3 38	..	..	..	..	5 55	..	..	..
3	Upton and Blewbury. ..	7 47	..	..	..	10 58	..	..	..	..	..	2 12	3 45	..	..	..	..	6 2	..	..	..
6¾	Churn	7 54	..	..	..	Aa	..	..	..	..	..	Aa	Aa	..	..	..	..	Aa	..	..	..
8½	Compton	7 59	..	..	..	11 11	..	..	..	..	..	2 23	3 56	..	..	..	..	6 14	..	..	..
10½	Hampstead Norris	8 4	..	..	..	11 17	..	..	..	..	..	2 30	4 1	..	..	..	..	6 20	..	..	..
12¾	Pinewood Halt	8 10	..	..	..	11 23	..	..	..	..	..	2 36	4 7	..	..	..	..	6 27	..	..	..
13½	Hermitage	8 13	..	..	..	11 27	..	..	..	..	..	2 39	4 10	..	..	..	..	6 32	..	..	..
18	**Newbury** .. .. .. arr	8 21	..	..	..	11 35	..	..	..	..	..	2 50	4 20	..	..	..	..	6 41	..	..	..
—	**62 London** (Pad.).... dep	..	7N30	..	..	..	10 18	..	..	..	..	..	2 35	..	..	..	..	..	..	6 0	..
—	**Newbury** .. .. .. dep	..	9 7	..	..	..	12 25	..	..	..	..		4 32	..		..	..	..	..	7 25	..
21¼	Woodhay	..	9 15	..	..	..	12 32	..	..	..	..		4 39	..		..	..	..	..	7 32	..
23½	Highclere	..	9 21	..	..	..	12 38	..	..	..	..		4 45	..		..	..	..	..	7 38	..
25½	Burghclere	..	9 26	..	..	..	12 43	..	..	..	..		4 49	..		..	..	..	..	7 42	..
28	Litchfield	..	9 32	..	..	..	12 49	..		..	..	Saturdays only	4 55	..	Except Saturdays	..	..	..	..	7 48	..
31¾	Whitchurch Town........	..	9 40	..	..	..	12 56	..	Commences 2nd May, 1960	..	..		5 3	..		..	..	..	..	7 56	..
37½	Sutton Scotney	..	9 51	..	..	..	1 7	..		..	..		5 14	..		..	..	..	..	8 7	..
40¼	Worthy Down Halt	..	9 58	..	..	..	1 14	..		..	..		5 21	..		..	..	..	..	8 14	..
42½	King's Worthy	..	10 3	..	..	..	1 19	..		..	..		5 25	..		..	..	..	..	8 18	..
44¼	**Winchester Chesil** arr	..	10 8	..	..	..	1 24	..		..	..		5 30	..		..	..	..	..	8 23	..
	dep	..	10 9	..	..	..	1 25	..		..	..		5 31	..		..	..	..	..	8 24	..
47¼	Shawford .... arr	..	..	..	..	..	..	..		..	..		5 39	..		..	..	..	..	..	..
51	**Eastleigh** .. .. arr	..	10 22	..	..	..	1 37	..	..	..	..		5 45	..		..	..	..	..	8 37	..
	dep	..	..	10 34	..	..	..	..	2 0	2 6	..	..	..	..	6 0	6 6	..	..	..	..	9 6
53¼	Swaythling .. .. .. arr	..	..	10 38	..	..	..	..	..	2 10	..	..	..	..	6 4	6 10	..	..	..	..	9 10
54¾	St Denys .... "	..	..	10 42	..	..	..	..	..	2 14	..	..	..	..	6 8	6 14	..	..	..	..	9 14
55¾	Northam .. .. .. "	..	..	10 44	..	..	..	..	..	2 16	..	..	..	..	6 10	6 16	..	..	..	..	9 16
56½	**Southampton Term.** "	..	..	10 47	..	..	..	..	..	2 19	..	..	..	..	6 13	6 19	..	..	..	..	9 19
56¾	**Southampton Cen.**. arr	..	..	..	..	..	..	..	2 10	..	..	..	..	..	..	..	..	..	..	..	..

Aa Stops to take up or set down on previous notice to Station Master at Didcot. Evening trains call during daylight only
B Arr 2 minutes *earlier*
C Arr 4 minutes *earlier*
E Except Saturdays
G Arr 3 minutes *earlier*

Kk Stops to take up or set down on previous notice to Station Master at Newbury. Evening trains call during daylight only
N Second class only for a portion of the journey
TC Through Carriages
Y On Saturdays arr 6 20 pm
Z On Saturdays arr 4 12 pm

On Sundays Bus services depart Didcot Station 3 0 pm to Newbury Station; returning from Newbury Station at 7 55 pm by Newbury and District Motor Services Ltd. Passengers holding rail tickets to or from stations between Didcot and Newbury inclusive may travel by these Road services without additional charge

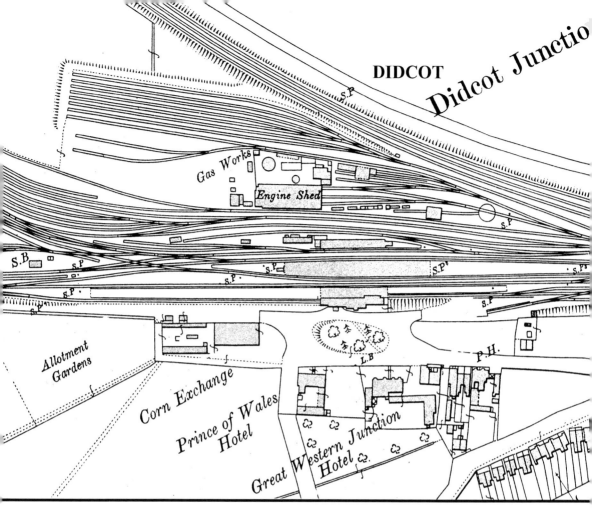

1. Opened in 1844, the station had a roof over four tracks until 1886. The station was rebuilt in 1892 when the main lines were quadrupled. Some tracks were altered again in 1932, when the Newbury bay (left) was provided with a loop and horse dock. On the right is the old engine shed. (LGRP)

The map has the London - Swindon line from right to left; the lowest of the five on the right is our route to Newbury. The curved track below it is Rich's engineering works siding. At the top are the avoiding lines to and from Oxford. The sidings below them were completely rearranged when a new engine shed was built in 1932.

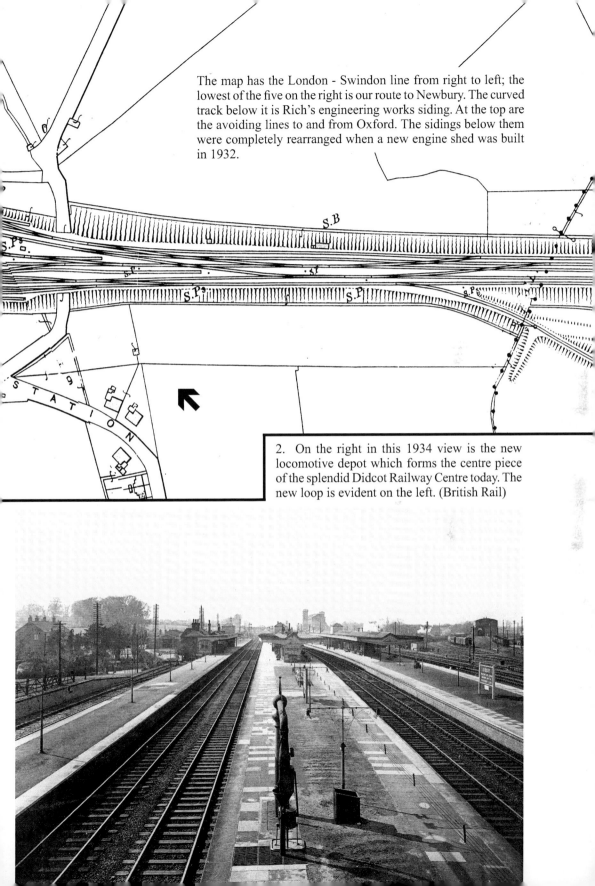

2. On the right in this 1934 view is the new locomotive depot which forms the centre piece of the splendid Didcot Railway Centre today. The new loop is evident on the left. (British Rail)

3. No. 3440 *City of Truro* stands at platform 1 with the 4.59pm from Southampton Terminus. Three coaches were a generous provision in the late 1950s. The through lines featured were used by fast trains. The quadrupling from London had been completed in 1892, as far as the junction at the west end of Didcot station. (Lens of Sutton)

June 1962

DIDCOT and NEWBURY

WEEK DAYS ONLY (Second class only, except where otherwise shown)

Miles		am		am		pm Z	pm	pm	Miles			am	pm	pm			pm Z	pm	
61	Oxford Z .. .. dep	7 10	..	10 5		1 30	3Y 0	5 5		Newbury .. .. .. dep		8 55	2 0	4 30	..		5 40	7 18	..
—	Didcot............. dep	7 40	....	10 50		2 15	3 36	5 58	4½	Hermitage		9 4	2 9	4 39	....		5 49	7 27	..
3	Upton and Blewbury ..	7 47	....	10 57		2 22	3 43	6 5	5½	Pinewood Halt		9 7	2 12	4 42	..		5 52	7 30	..
6¼	Churn	7 54	....	Aa		Aa	Aa	Aa	7½	Hampstead Norris.......		9 13	2 17	4 47	....		5 58	7 36	....
8¼	Compton	7 59	....	11 8		2 33	3 55	6 18	9¼	Compton		9 18	2 22	4 52	..		6 3	7 41	..
10¼	Hampstead Norris.......	8 4	....	11 13		2 38	4 0	6 24	11¼	Churn		Kk	Kk	Kk	....		Kk	Kk	
12¼	Pinewood Halt	8 10	..	11 19		2 44	4 6	6 30	15	Upton and Blewbury ..		9 28	2 32	5 2	..		6 13	7 51	..
13¼	Hermitage	8 13	....	11 22		2 47	4 9	6 34	18	Didcot............. arr		9 34	2 38	5 8	....		6 19	7 57	....
18	Newbury .. .. .. arr	8 21	..	11 B 30		2 55	4 17	6 42	28¼	61 Oxford Z .. .. arr		10 13	3X 0	5Y 34	..		6 50	9 33	..

Aa Stops to take up or set down on previous notice to Station Master at Didcot. Evening trains call during daylight only

ß On Saturdays arr 11 32 am

Kk Stops to take up or set down on previous notice to Station Master at Newbury. Evening trains call during daylight only

V On Saturdays arr 5 36 pm
X On Saturdays arr 3 48 pm
Y On Saturdays dep 3 5 pm
Z First and Second class

On Sundays Bus services operated by the Thames Valley Traction Company Ltd. depart Didcot Station 3 0 pm to Newbury Station; returning from Newbury Station at 7 55 pm

Passengers holding rail tickets to or from stations between Didcot and Newbury inclusive may travel by these Road services without additional charge

4. The 150-lever Didcot East Box dated from the 1932 alterations. The token is for the Newbury single line, which curves to the right on the embankment in the distance. The box closed on 17th May 1965, when the area was transferred to Reading Panel. (British Rail)

For other views of this station see
Didcot to Banbury
Didcot to Swindon
and Reading to Didcot

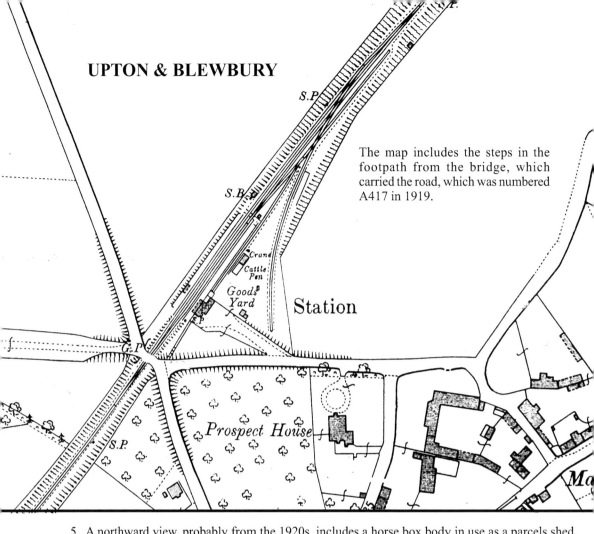

UPTON & BLEWBURY

S.P.

S.B.

The map includes the steps in the footpath from the bridge, which carried the road, which was numbered A417 in 1919.

Crane

Cattle Pen

Goods Yard

Station

G.P.

Prospect House

S.P.

Ma

5. A northward view, probably from the 1920s, includes a horse box body in use as a parcels shed, a down passenger train and an up goods. This building plan was used at the majority of the stations on the route. (J.M.Butterfield)

6. The only access to the up platform was via the foot crossing seen in this and the previous picture. It was more dangerous after the track doubling. On the crumbling concrete post is the winch for a pressurised oil lamp, known as the Tilley. (Lens of Sutton)

Upton and Blewbury	1903	1913	1923	1933
Passenger tickets issued	4781	6116	6681	5173
Season tickets issued	*	4	33	10
Parcels forwarded	4776	3818	2928	4393
General goods forwarded (tons)	1702	1687	1400	231
Coal and coke received (tons)	20	13	76	123
Other minerals received (tons)	801	664	802	376
General goods received (tons)	336	485	881	244
Trucks of livestock handled	24	23	33	39
(* not available)				

7. Evident here is that access to the yard was from the up line and that the horse box had been replaced by an asbestos-clad shed. Why was it fitted with a stove? The main building survives as a private house and is now surrounded by other dwellings. (M.Hale)

→ 8. "Blewbury" was added to the station name on 16th January 1911 and a porch was added to the signal box in the 1920s. From 1943 to 1949, there were intermediate block signals at Ilsley, about halfway to Compton. (I.D.Beale)

→ 9. The yard once loaded many racehorses but by the 1950s sugar beet outwards and coal inwards for the Harwell Atomic Energy Research Establishment were the notable traffics. All ceased on 10th August 1964. The crane is visible; this was of only one-ton capacity. (J.H.Moss)

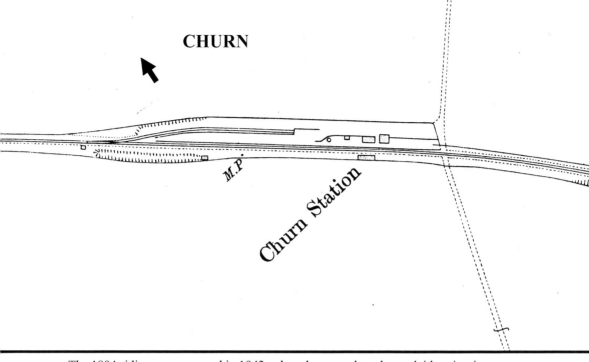

CHURN

Churn Station

M.P.

The 1894 siding was removed in 1942, when the second track was laid on its site.

10. A platform was provided here in June 1888 for the benefit of the National Rifle Association and was used subsequently by many annual military camps. There was no road access. No. 3206 *Earl of Plymouth* is climbing south in about 1937. (D.Thompson)

11. A closer look at the platform in single line days reveals only a hut, a urinal and an occupation crossing. The posts are devoid of lamps, timetables stating that trains would not call after dark. The original wooden building had been destroyed by fire in 1924. (D.Thompson)

12. The third building was a double-sided shelter, erected in 1943. *City of Truro* speeds south through the desolate and windswept landscape, requests to stop here having been required since 1931. There is little trace here today. (H.Davis)

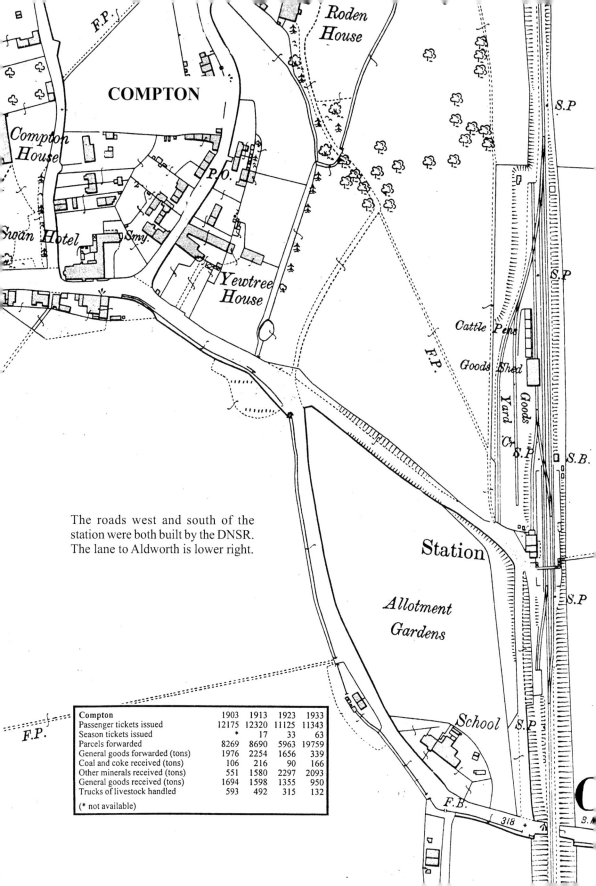

The roads west and south of the station were both built by the DNSR. The lane to Aldworth is lower right.

Compton	1903	1913	1923	1933
Passenger tickets issued	12175	12320	11125	11343
Season tickets issued	*	17	33	63
Parcels forwarded	8269	8690	5963	19759
General goods forwarded (tons)	1976	2254	1656	339
Coal and coke received (tons)	106	216	90	166
Other minerals received (tons)	551	1580	2297	2093
General goods received (tons)	1694	1598	1355	950
Trucks of livestock handled	593	492	315	132

(* not available)

13. The coalman's horse was sometimes used to move wagons in the yard but would not normally appear on the main line. Tiled platform canopies were provided initially at most of the stations, as were flat-bottom rails. (G.Ludlow)

14. One load of sand is the only evidence of revenue behind this 6100 class on 14th March 1953. In the background is the yard's three-ton crane. Also visible is the replacement semi-glazed canopy. The building is now a private house. (T.B.Sands)

15. Drifting into the up platform on 27th June 1959 is ex-LSWR class T9 no. 30117. The dock had once been busy with horses from the nearby racing stables. (D.Fereday Glenn)

16. Southbound is ex-GWR no. 2246 with ex-SR coaches of Bulleid's design. The goods yard was often the busiest on the route north of Winchester, access being possible from either line. (E.Wilmshurst)

17. The footbridge was the only one at an intermediate station on the route and was provided to carry a public footpath. The first was of timber construction, the second is seen in picture 13; this is the final form, cast in concrete. The shed was erected in 1927 for milk traffic. (Lens of Sutton)

18. Pannier tanks were usually confined to local trains north of Newbury. Few wooden signal posts lasted to the end of the line. The goods yard was once busy with iron inwards for T.Baker's foundry and their carts and ploughs outwards. The yard closed on 10th August 1964. (D.Fereday Glenn)

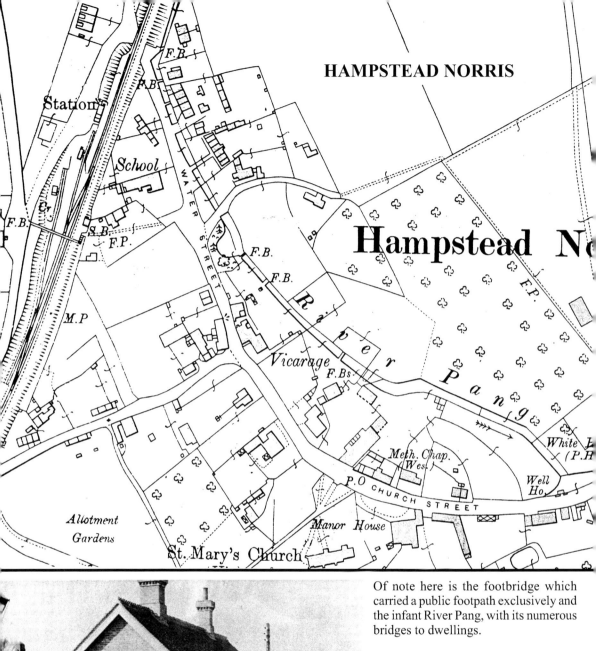

HAMPSTEAD NORRIS

Station

School

F.B.

F.B.

F.B.

F.B.

F.P.

Hampstead N

WATER STREET

M.P

Vicarage

F.Bs.

River Pang

White

(P.H

Meth. Chap.
(Wes.)

Well
Ho.

P.O. CHURCH STREET

Allotment
Gardens

Manor House

St. Mary's Church

Of note here is the footbridge which carried a public footpath exclusively and the infant River Pang, with its numerous bridges to dwellings.

19. The station was unusual in being a single storey structure and devoid of a canopy. There was no accommodation for the station master either. At least the village was close to hand. (R. Wilkinson coll.)

20. The original crane fell into disuse and, when a Naval store was established nearby, a mobile crane was brought to the yard when necessary. (A.E.Smith)

21. The 11.20am to Newbury was recorded at the 1942 platform on 7th September 1959. The first signal box was down graded to a ground frame at an early date. In 1920, most of the box was moved onto the platform (left) to serve as a parcels shed, as there had been an increase in poultry traffic. (E.T.Gill)

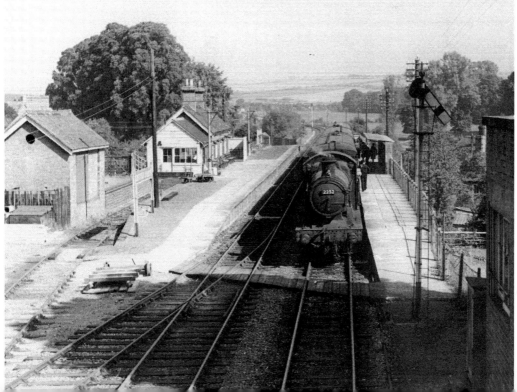

← 22. The long public footbridge had been added in 1883 but few other alterations were made, other than the doubling. Agricultural traffic was important here but was about half the volume of that handled at Compton.
(Lens of Sutton)

Hampstead Norris	1903	1913	1923	1933
Passenger tickets issued	7368	9588	9776	7264
Season tickets issued	*	25	42	45
Parcels forwarded	2093	8352	12286	6437
General goods forwarded (tons)	1093	1179	1242	305
Coal and coke received (tons)	221	163	102	317
Other minerals received (tons)	377	810	868	3704
General goods received (tons)	1091	1534	1073	538
Trucks of livestock handled	25	46	65	43
(* not available)				

← 23. A southward view from the footbridge reveals the long rodding run required after the second track (left) was brought into use in February 1943. The yard handled coal only after 19th May 1964 until line closure. (T.B.Sands)

24. The horse dock beyond the goods shed was built in 1928 and was busy with racehorses until the 1950s. The signal box (right) was the only wartime type to be built north of Newbury. There is no trace of the railway here now.
(Lens of Sutton)

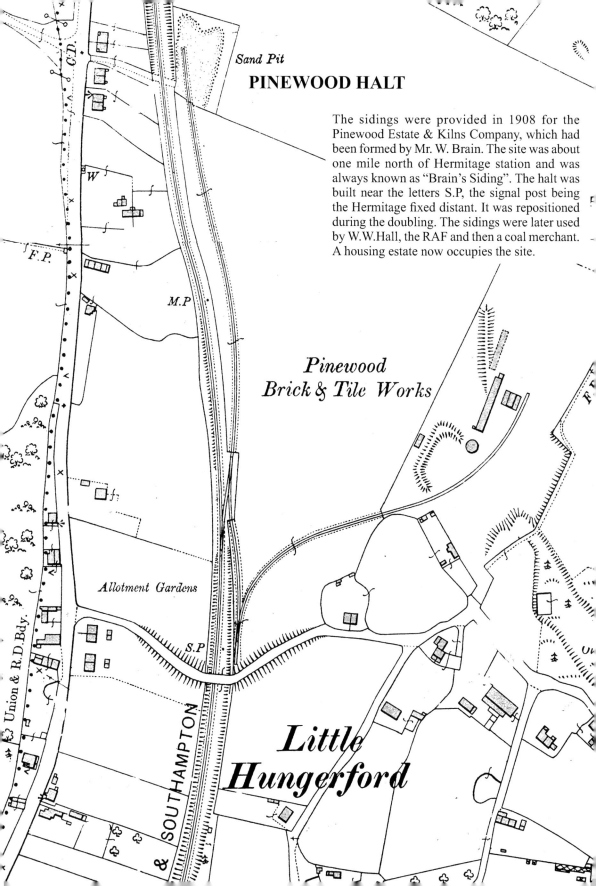

Sand Pit

PINEWOOD HALT

The sidings were provided in 1908 for the Pinewood Estate & Kilns Company, which had been formed by Mr. W. Brain. The site was about one mile north of Hermitage station and was always known as "Brain's Siding". The halt was built near the letters S.P, the signal post being the Hermitage fixed distant. It was repositioned during the doubling. The sidings were later used by W.W.Hall, the RAF and then a coal merchant. A housing estate now occupies the site.

Pinewood Brick & Tile Works

W

M.P

F.P.

G.N.

Allotment Gardens

S.P

Union & R.D.Bdy.

SOUTHAMPTON &

Little Hungerford

25. A southward view shows the original platform and hut on the right. These had been brought into use on 11th September 1933 and served the northern part of the village of Hermitage. (Lens of Sutton)

26. Looking south in 1960, we see one of the two pairs of gateposts on the private sidings. Arriving passengers had to travel in the compartments next to the guards van; those departing had to buy tickets at the next station. (R.M.Casserley)

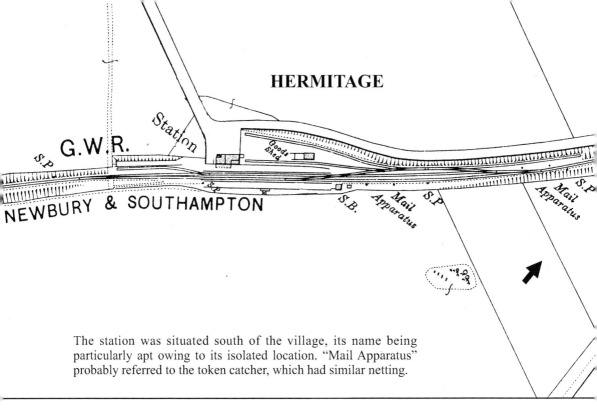

HERMITAGE

G.W.R.

Station

Goods Shed

NEWBURY & SOUTHAMPTON

S.P.

S.P.

S.B.

Mail Apparatus

S.P

Mail Apparatus

S.P.

The station was situated south of the village, its name being particularly apt owing to its isolated location. "Mail Apparatus" probably referred to the token catcher, which had similar netting.

27. A northward panorama in the 1930s includes the original round point rodding and the then new posts for Tilley lamps. Parcels abound - covered space was limited. The building is now a private dwelling. (Mowat coll.)

28. The signal box porch was an afterthought and the adjacent PW hut was erected during World War II, when the track to be maintained doubled and train weights increased. The local population was under 700. (I.D.Beale)

29. Class 6100 2-6-2T no. 6134 is northbound as civilian and military passengers wait for their train. In the background is the large food store erected by the Government in 1943. (T.B.Sands)

Hermitage	1903	1913	1923	1933
Passenger tickets issued	12027	14144	13631	9767
Season tickets issued	*	51	49	31
Parcels forwarded	4288	7033	9033	7639
General goods forwarded (tons)	2860	1932	1684	502
Coal and coke received (tons)	519	378	257	348
Other minerals received (tons)	354	2094	1005	3147
General goods received (tons)	1391	1404	1121	583
Trucks of livestock handled	161	126	17	28
(* not available)				

30. Taken a few minutes later, the goods train has set back into the long refuge siding (added in 1943) in order not to delay the following passenger train from Newbury. Hidden by the wagons is a loop and two sidings provided for the food store. On the right is the dock shown on the map. (T.B.Sands)

31. The station, but not the sign, appears freshly painted in this May 1961 photograph. White bands on the stanchions persist, although these were applied during the blackout of World War II. (M.Hale)

SOUTH OF HERMITAGE

32. The number of fully braked freight trains gradually increased during the 1950s. Running times were reduced but shunting times increased. Class 2800 2-8-0 no. 3809 is southbound and its train passes over Fishers Lane level crossing, one of only two on the route. (G.Gore)

33. Newbury East Junction fixed distant arm warns the driver to act with caution, as he rounds the curve leading to the main line. The D6500s became class 33. This section is now part of an industrial estate. (G.Gore)

34. The down line from Didcot is on the left as no. 2221 (right) runs towards Newbury Racecourse station, which is beyond the bridge in the background. The two tracks on the right served this station and were also used for goods trains. In the centre of this 1958 picture are no. 7923 *Speke Hall*, a "Castle" class and Newbury East Box. (A.C.Ingram)

NEWBURY

35. The GWR forced the DNSR to pay for an expensive rebuilding of the station and provision of through lines, as the former contended that the latter's trains were delaying their expresses. This is the north elevation soon after its completion in 1910; it is little altered today. (Unknown)

36. This bridge is seen in the background of the previous picture and was photographed as the new platform was being finished in 1910. The new Middle Box is also included. The original station had a roof over the tracks; a similar one can still be seen at Frome and is featured in our *Frome to Bristol* album. (British Rail)

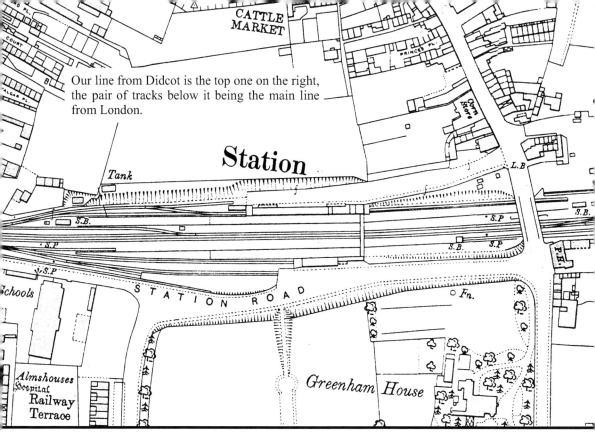

Our line from Didcot is the top one on the right, the pair of tracks below it being the main line from London.

37. The goods yard was so busy in the steam era that a locomotive was often shunting all day, many local goods trains being reformed here. A marine engine from nearby Plenty & Sons was pictured in the 1940s, the view including the jib of the 7-ton crane which was situated close to the goods shed. (British Rail)

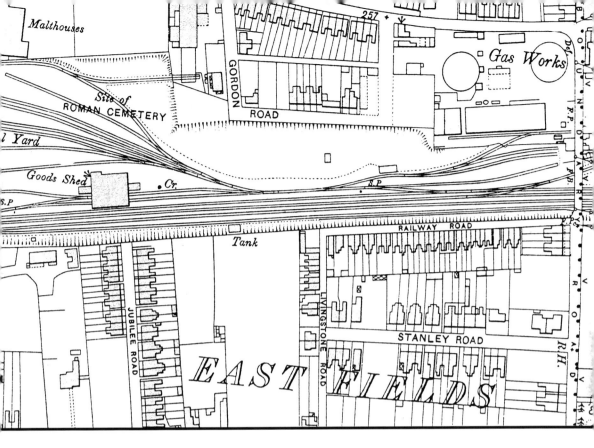

38. No. 5921 is leaving the down bay with a local train for Westbury. Didcot-Southampton trains commonly stopped in the down through platform while the locomotive took water and the passengers alighted. It then moved into the bay to await a connection from London. The horse dock is on the right; the other siding was often used for carriage berthing. (Unknown)

39. A Lambourn branch train is featured in this eastward view, the other train probably being bound for the Winchester line. Both bay areas have been converted to car parks. (D.W.Winkworth)

40. No. 6302 waits to depart for Didcot on 5th March 1960, the last day of service from Winchester. The adjacent bay had been used by local trains to Didcot and was retained for use by some stopping trains to London. All three signal boxes closed in 1978 - East on 20th March, Middle on 4th March and West on 16th April. (R.A.Lissenden)

ENBORNE JUNCTION

41. A class T9 4-4-0 curves away from the main line and starts the four mile climb to Highclere. The signals include one for the up goods loop which was added during WWII. The Newbury bypass has been built in this vicinity. (J.S.Gilks)

42. The signal box and junction signals are in the background as no. 34076 *41 Squadron* tackles the 1 in 106 gradient. The "Battle of Britain" class was seldom photographed on the route as its members were only used on it on freight trains in the final years. The box closed on 29th January 1967. (G.Gore)

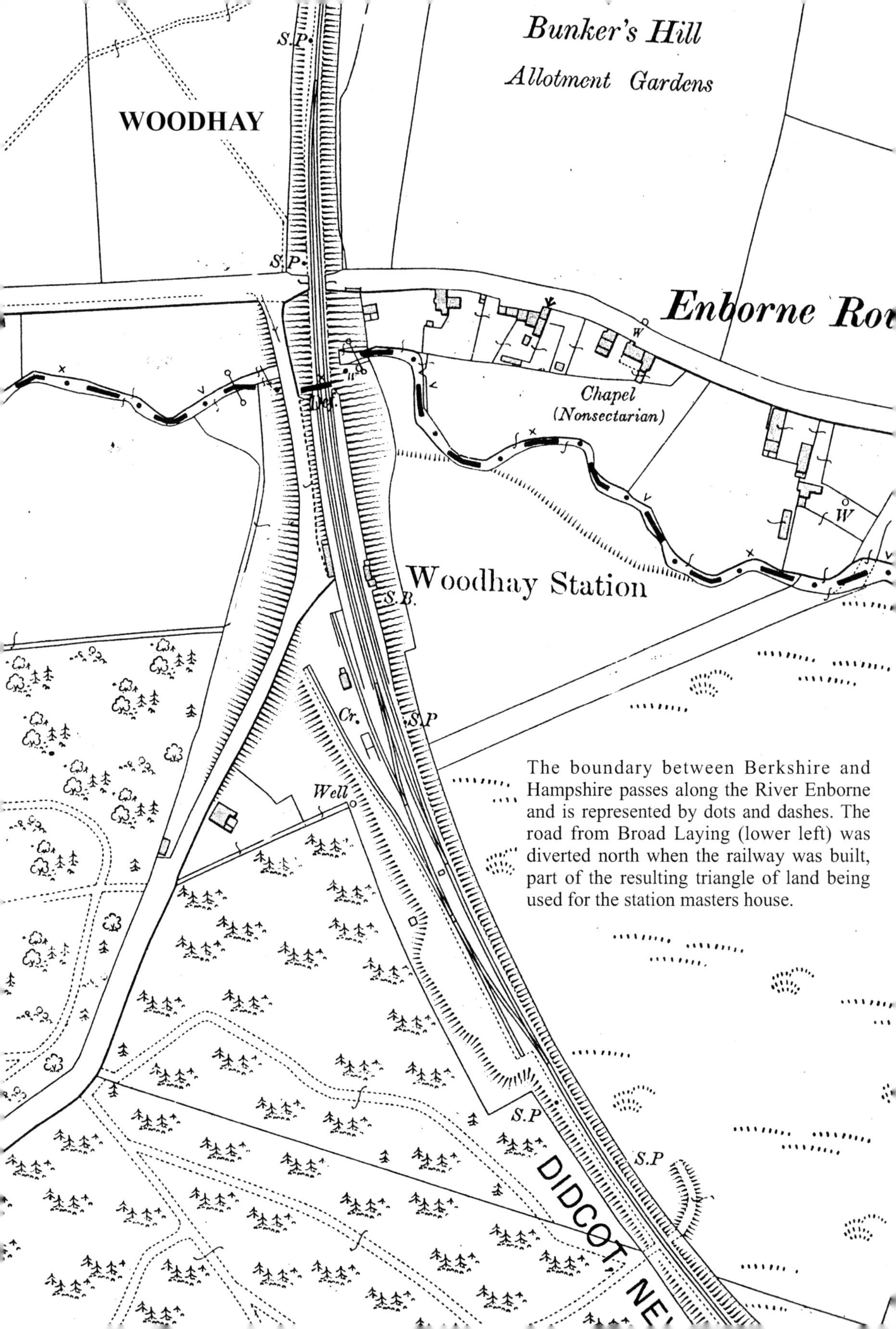

WOODHAY

Bunker's Hill

Allotment Gardens

Enborne Row

Chapel
(Nonsectarian)

W

W

Woodhay Station

S.B.

S.P

Cr.

Well

The boundary between Berkshire and
Hampshire passes along the River Enborne
and is represented by dots and dashes. The
road from Broad Laying (lower left) was
diverted north when the railway was built,
part of the resulting triangle of land being
used for the station masters house.

S.P

S.P

DIDCOT NE

43. A southward panorama includes the 16-lever original signal box and the 1915 bicycle shed, which was necessary as the station served a scattered community of over 1500. Passenger figures were often second only to Winchester. (D.Thompson)

44. No. 3210 was a regular performer on the line and was recorded running towards the platform in 1948. Didcot and Winchester locomotive crews often changed trains at this station. (G.L.Hoare)

Woodhay	1903	1913	1923	1933
Passenger tickets issued	18422	20011	12269	2869
Season tickets issued	*	*	17	22
Parcels forwarded	5829	9373	10800	7059
General goods forwarded (tons)	763	1857	602	#
Coal and coke received (tons)	456	290	391	#
Other minerals received (tons)	654	349	2327	#
General goods received (tons)	2199	1267	860	#
Trucks of livestock handled	11	3	20	#
# Controlled by Newbury from Nov 1st 1932				
(* not available)				

45. Timber was usually chosen as the material for construction of stations sited on embankments, owing to lower weight and inability to crack with movement. Coal was the principal goods inwards and pit props were high on the list outwards. (E.Wilmshurst)

46. Another regular engine on the route was "Bulldog" class 4-4-0 no. 3448 *Kingfisher*, a class that was introduced in 1898. Didcot shed provided all the locomotives for the route until the final years. (G.L.Hoare)

47. The second signal box was at the southern end of the double track section and was opened on 9th October 1942. This 1960 southward view includes the lines to the goods yard, which closed on 31st December 1962. (E.Wilmshurst)

48. A 1961 photograph includes the 3-ton crane and the original goods shed. The signs had gone and an air of dereliction had set in at this charming rural location. (M.Hale)

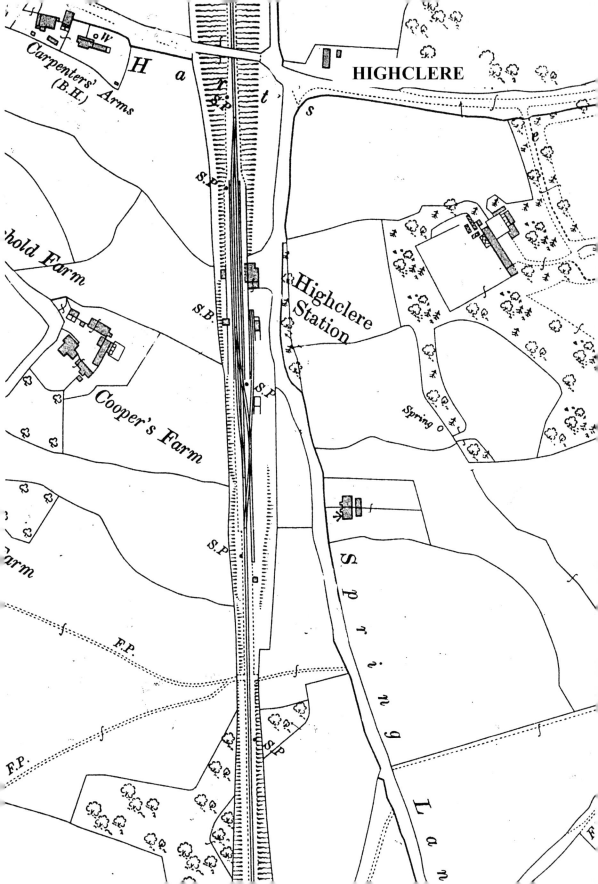

HIGHCLERE

Carpenters'
Arms
(B.H.)

hold Farm

Cooper's Farm

Highclere
Station

Spring o

Spring Lane

Farm

F.P.

F.P.

← Curiously Highclere station was close to Burghclere and Woodhay was the most convenient one for Highclere. However, most of the route is now under the new controversial alignment of the A34. The crane (Cr.) was of 3-ton capacity.

Highclere	1903	1913	1923	1933
Passenger tickets issued	8983	8341	7503	3399
Season tickets issued	*	*	13	2
Parcels forwarded	4572	6356	7483	4219
General goods forwarded (tons)	427	306	155	#
Coal and coke received (tons)	84	96	213	#
Other minerals received (tons)	40	53	678	#
General goods received (tons)	606	411	275	#
Trucks of livestock handled	17	4	3	#

Controlled by Newbury from Nov 1st 1932
(* not available)

49. Looking south from the road bridge, we can observe the white painted cattle pens, the well tended flower beds, the close proximity of the oil lamps, the shortness of the loop and the partly obscured signal box.
(Lens of Sutton)

← 50. The loop was lengthened in about 1922 and is seen in the 1930s along with larger radius points. The thick white posts carry token catchers. (Mowat coll.)

← 51. The old A34 passed over the line north of the station on a frail lattice girder bridge, which had a weight restriction of a mere *seven* tons. To accommodate wartime road traffic, it was fitted with a timber trestle support in 1942. A short tunnel had been built here but it collapsed before being completed. The loop had been extended further north in 1942. Southbound is an Eastleigh based T9. (T.B.Sands)

52. No. 76013 was almost new when photographed near the cattle dock in 1953, awaiting the passing of an up train. The single point rod worked the yard points; the loop points beyond the bridge were electrically operated. (T.B.Sands)

53. The original signal box was replaced by this standard wartime box, which was situated at the south end of the loop. The token apparatus is near the 18th lever. On the right is a hand-operated generator for the point motors. (Westinghouse Signal Co.)

➜ 54. A local lady makes her last shopping trip by train on 4th March 1960. The canopies south of Newbury were never tiled. The goods yard remained in use until 31st December 1962, the shed eventually being converted to a garage to serve the house that was created from the main building. (D.Cross)

➜ 55. Leaking badly, class 4300 no. 6302 was recorded with an up train on the last day of passenger service, 5th March 1960. It is on the down line as the loop and signal box had been taken out of use on 6th February 1955. (A.E.Bennett)

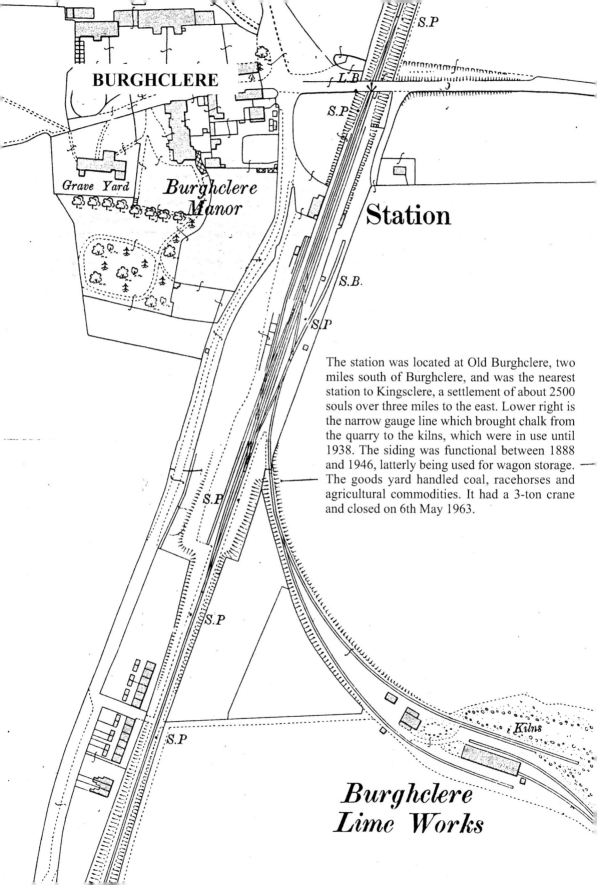

BURGHCLERE

Grave Yard

Burghclere Manor

S.P

L.B

S.P

Station

S.B.

S.P

S.P

S.P

S.P

The station was located at Old Burghclere, two miles south of Burghclere, and was the nearest station to Kingsclere, a settlement of about 2500 souls over three miles to the east. Lower right is the narrow gauge line which brought chalk from the quarry to the kilns, which were in use until 1938. The siding was functional between 1888 and 1946, latterly being used for wagon storage. The goods yard handled coal, racehorses and agricultural commodities. It had a 3-ton crane and closed on 6th May 1963.

Kilns

Burghclere Lime Works

56. An early northward view shows the unsupported canopy (typical of stations from here southwards) and the short loop. This was lengthened in November 1942, the cutting having to be widened on the left. The main buildings survive. (Mrs J.Ford)

57. A southward panorama includes the summit of the southern section in the distance, the limeworks on the left, steps to the down platform (which provided a direct path for pedestrians from Kingsclere) and an up shunt signal. (Mowat coll.)

Burghclere	1903	1913	1923	1933
Passenger tickets issued	7975	8349	5656	3078
Season tickets issued	*	*	23	3
Parcels forwarded	3511	3100	4343	1621
General goods forwarded (tons)	962	580	662	#
Coal and coke received (tons)	1604	443	624	#
Other minerals received (tons)	206	57	1654	#
General goods received (tons)	1592	1600	1102	#
Trucks of livestock handled	8	33	29	#

Controlled by Newbury from Nov 1st 1932
(* not available)

58. The original 16-lever signal box seen in the previous view was replaced by this object. It was sited further south. The limeworkers cottages in the background are lower left on the map. The driver collects the token, while the signalman walks towards the catcher. (F.E.Brown)

59. With so many men called for war service, women were recruited for various duties, such as porters. Few were considered suitable for signalling and most were sacked when the men returned. However, Bessie Sherman retained her post and retired in March 1960. (R.A.Lissenden)

60. A shady glade, a lady in the grass and a beautiful T9 - bliss. We say no more. (E.C.Griffiths)

61. Class U no. 31794 waits for a clear road as nos. 76011 (class 4) and 31795 (class U) run north with loaded oil tankers on 5th March 1960. Double heading was probably due to the non-availability of the usual class 9F 2-10-0. (D.Fereday Glenn)

← 62. A through Paddington to Southampton train was recorded on the descent to Litchfield around the turn of the century. (M.Snellgrove coll.)

64. In the background is the bulk of Beacon Hill as no. 2241 descends the long incline towards Litchfield. (M.Esau)

← 63. A northbound train, with a through coach to London at the rear, was photographed in about 1900, by a bicycling cameraman. (M.Snellgrove coll.)

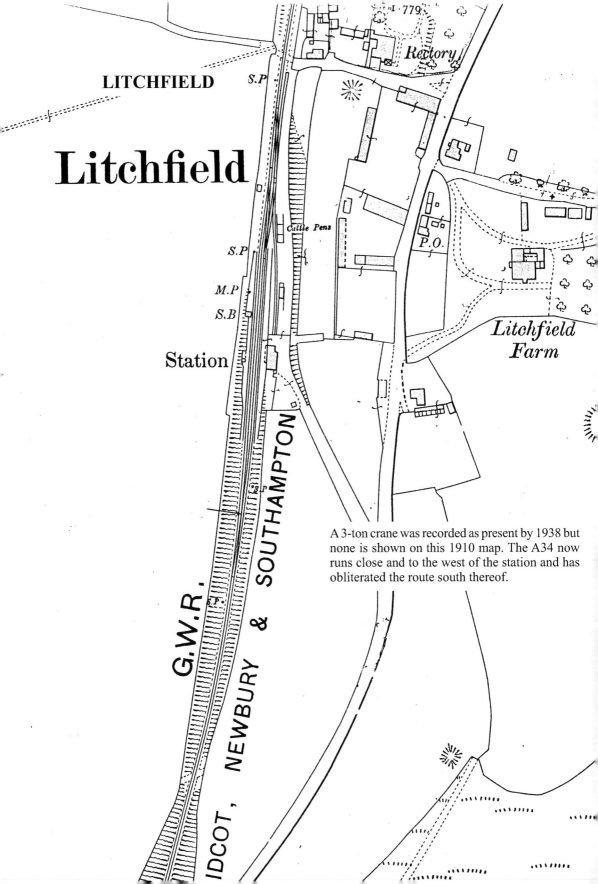

LITCHFIELD

S.P

Litchfield

Rectory

S.P

Cattle Pens

S.P

M.P

S.B

P.O.

Station

Litchfield
Farm

G.W.R.

IDCOT, NEWBURY & SOUTHAMPTON

A 3-ton crane was recorded as present by 1938 but none is shown on this 1910 map. The A34 now runs close and to the west of the station and has obliterated the route south thereof.

65. The original loop and signal box were taken out of use on 5th July 1936. A new box (left) and a longer loop were brought into traffic in March 1943. No. 3212 is approaching the platforms from the north. (G.H.Robin)

66. Class 4300 2-6-0 no. 6313 is departing south beside the rusty rails of the up loop, which had ceased to be used on 23rd January 1955 at which time the signal box closed. (Lens of Sutton)

67. The goods yard remained open until 13th August 1962, the points being worked from the ground frame partly visible on the right. Class 4 4-6-0 no. 75005 is northbound with assorted coaches. (T.Wright)

Litchfield	1903	1913	1923	1933
Passenger tickets issued	3552	4631	4233	2194
Season tickets issued	*	*	11	2
Parcels forwarded	2500	2321	2858	1308
General goods forwarded (tons)	962	653	583	#
Coal and coke received (tons)	9	105	30	#
Other minerals received (tons)	38	177	2048	#
General goods received (tons)	368	571	565	#
Trucks of livestock handled	5	39	43	#

Controlled by Newbury from Nov 1st 1932
(* not available)

68. Running south in February 1960 is a train composed mainly of empty oil tankers. The demand for oil products increased enormously in that decade. (E.Wilmshurst)

69. The station gardens had once won prizes; that was when there was a staff of two men and a boy. The end is nigh. After years of dereliction, the building became a dwelling. (Lens of Sutton)

SOUTH OF LITCHFIELD

70. Chalk having a good angle of repose, the walls of the cuttings were left almost vertical. However, part broke away and fell into a passing carriage, necessitating temporary line closure. (E.A.Sollars)

71. Works trains were operated on Sundays for months, with or without butterfly collectors, to reprofile the cuttings. (E.A.Sollars)

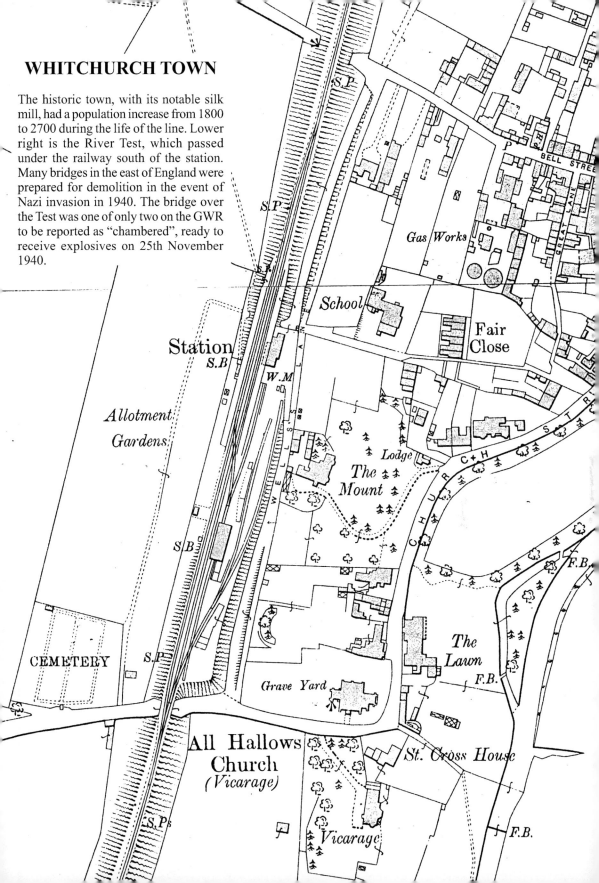

WHITCHURCH TOWN

The historic town, with its notable silk mill, had a population increase from 1800 to 2700 during the life of the line. Lower right is the River Test, which passed under the railway south of the station. Many bridges in the east of England were prepared for demolition in the event of Nazi invasion in 1940. The bridge over the Test was one of only two on the GWR to be reported as "chambered", ready to receive explosives on 25th November 1940.

S.P.

BELL STREET

GREAT LANE

Gas Works

School

Fair Close

Station

S.B

W.M

Allotment Gardens

Lodge

The Mount

C+H

CHURCH

RIVER TEST

F.B.

S.B

The Lawn

F.B.

CEMETERY

S.P.

Grave Yard

All Hallows Church
(Vicarage)

St. Cross House

F.B.

S.P.

Vicarage

F.B.

72. A northward view reveals that the up shelter was unlike the others, being devoid of a canopy owing to the signalman's viewing requirements. Again there are ornamental barge boards and vallance. (Lens of Sutton)

73. The station's elevated position above the town is evident, as is the gasworks which provided station lighting. (E.Moss coll.)

74. The nameboard carries the suffix "Hants", which was added on 1st July 1924, following the grouping of the railways. It was changed to "Town" on 26th September 1949. The small building in the distance accommodated an eight-lever ground frame. (Mowat coll.)

75. The loop was lengthened at its north end in 1943. A water column and an auxillary token instrument cupboard were provided near the starting signal. The Waterloo-Exeter line is in the background. Evidence of the proposed connection between the two routes and views of Whitchurch North are in our *Basingstoke to Salisbury* album. (British Rail)

← 76. Two 1956 photographs include ex-LSWR engines based at Eastleigh and were amongst other Southern Region locomotives used on the route after April 1950. The top of the inclined path to the subway is to the left of the smokebox of class T9 no. 30288. (M.Esau)

Whitchurch	1903	1913	1923	1933
Passenger tickets issued	15387	17737	15804	4968
Season tickets issued	*	*	16	7
Parcels forwarded	5987	6681	5153	5480
General goods forwarded (tons)	725	1560	713	+
Coal and coke received (tons)	1343	400	24	+
Other minerals received (tons)	621	3038	1393	+
General goods received (tons)	1511	3739	1704	+
Trucks of livestock handled	46	168	29	+

+ Included with Winchester from 1932 to 1935
(* not available)

77. No. 30283 is northbound and the 1943 signal box is in the background. The water tank that appears in both photographs was erected in 1943 to give a good supply for wartime traffic. The old tank was supplied with river water by a gas engine-driven pump. (M.Esau)

78. Class U no. 31803 is working "wrong road" on 23rd January 1960, owing to a points motor failure. The goods yard once loaded quantities of watercress, lettuce, cucumber and jam, mainly for Midland markets. It closed on 9th May 1963. The main building only survives, in use as a dwelling. (E.Wilmshurst)

← 79. Signalman Ken Alexander demands the return of the token after the unorthodox arrival of class 4 2-6-0 no. 76017 on 23rd September 1954. The 7.0am "fast goods" from Banbury had been carrying bricks and timber and ran out of control. The crew jumped clear and the up passenger train stopped 70 yds away, with timber scattered widely. (K.Alexander coll.)

← 80. The accident occurred at about 11.0am but the line was clear by 5.45pm. However, the locomotive retained its inelegant posture for another week. Here was another example of the problems of working "unfitted" freight trains over long steep gradients and also the benefit of catch points. (S.C.Townroe)

81. There was a repeat performance on 12th February 1960, when no. 76026 jettisoned its dome cover, and two wagons were forced onto their ends. The fireman was injured and an approaching light engine stopped in time. (S.C.Townroe)

SUTTON SCOTNEY

This is the 1941 edition and includes the longer bridge provided in 1937 for the A30, also the new wide road to the left of it. (The narrow street below the place name had previously been the A30.) The weighing machine (W.M.) had been installed in 1907.

Brightlands

R o a d

Saddlers Arms (P.H.)

Sutton Scotney

Mill House

Fish Pond

Tennis Court

Recreation

Pavilion

F.B.

S.B.

W.M.

Sutton S Stat

Methodist Church

St. Luke's Church

White Swan Inn

Victoria Hall

The Avenue

War Memorial

82. Tank engines were not a common sight on the route, although some were used as far as Newbury in various periods. The footbridge carried a footpath and was erected in 1886. (Unknown)

83. A "Barnum" class 2-4-0 waits with an up train, while the rules are broken and a porter throws an empty box across the down track. Compare the track layout with that shown in the previous picture. (Unknown)

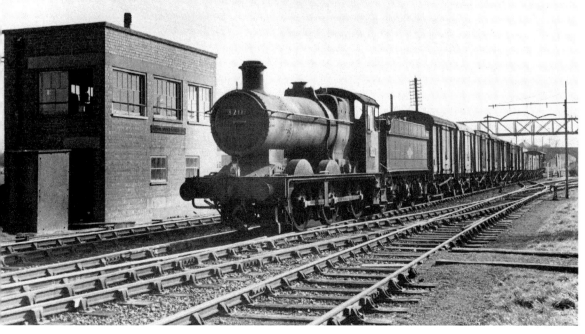

84. A splendid photograph from the 1930s includes the weigh-house, two end-lettered cattle trucks, the original signal box and the small parcels shed that had covered a ground frame at the north end of the yard until about 1922. (T.Palmer)

Sutton Scotney	1903	1913	1923	1933
Passenger tickets issued	12515	14694	10758	4022
Season tickets issued	*	*	26	-
Parcels forwarded	4132	7213	9307	5083
General goods forwarded (tons)	1423	2438	1734	+
Coal and coke received (tons)	518	561	312	+
Other minerals received (tons)	2862	1747	3230	+
General goods received (tons)	2105	2154	1466	+
Trucks of livestock handled	59	197	157	+

+ Included with Winchester from 1932 to 1935
(* not available)

85. A northbound goods rattles past the 1943 signal box on 4th March 1960, hauled by 2200 class no. 3211. Note that wartime track alterations included providing yard access from the down loop again. It had loaded pigs, hops, strawberries and grain, finally ceasing activity on 3rd February 1964. (D.Cross)

86. The signalman obscures the full length of the loop as the driver of no. 76011 waits to depart north. He will soon pass the site of Lodge Bridge loop, which was in use from March 1943 until March 1950. The station area was cleared and occupied by a firm of civil engineers. (P.J.Cupper)

87. Although the route had been constructed to receive double track, chalk falls in the cuttings eventually reduced the space by half. Class T9 no. 30117 is running north with rail enthusiasts on 30th April 1961. The tour from Waterloo ran via Portsmouth Harbour, Droxford, Gosport, Southampton Central, Eastleigh, Newbury and Ascot. (M.Esau)

➔ 88. A platform and two sidings were completed at War Office expense in October 1917 for use by the Royal Flying Corps. The platform was available for public use from 1st April 1918 and a horse box body was provided as a booking office. The loop and signal box are seen under construction in 1943. The old platform was soon to be removed and a new island type provided. The curious two-ton crane was of military origin. (British Rail)

WORTHY DOWN HALT

89. The two original sidings were loops and were replaced by this single siding, which remained in use until 1953. In both wars there were extensions into nearby camps. (Lens of Sutton)

The signalling diagram reveals that the box controlled the 1943 connection from the SR main line.

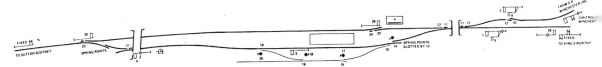

90. The basic booking office can be seen to the left of the signal box in the previous picture. The signalman issued the tickets. (T.B.Sands)

91. The north end of the loop was recorded on 16th July 1963, as empty oil tanks are returned from the Midlands to the South Coast refineries. This was the proposed site of a station for Winchester Racecourse in the 1890s. (P.H.Swift)

92. There was very limited civilian traffic at this bleak location but the arrival of the 11.30pm from Winchester on wartime Saturday evenings

created a busy and noisy scene. The top brickwork had been rendered due to water penetration, a common problem with the 1943 boxes. (L.Elsey)

SOUTH OF WORTHY DOWN

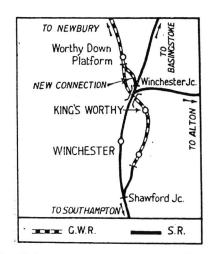

The connection between the SR and GWR was completed in 1943 and was intended to ease the flow of south-north military traffic by avoiding conflicting movements at Shawford Junction. (Railway Magazine)

93. The single line connection at Winchester Junction is seen as a Waterloo to Southampton train speeds south. The signal box can be found in picture 63 in *Branch Lines to Alton* - Middleton Press. (J.L.Farrer)

94. This 1953 photograph is from the connection that had been disused since November 1951, apart from wagon storage. We are looking towards the parallel track to Worthy Down, with the line from Winchester Chesil on the left. (T.B.Sands)

95. Springvale Road passed under the line near the end of the train shown in the next picture. Class U no. 31807 and class 4 2-6-0 no. 76002 are climbing hard on 14th April 1960, the obligatory two empty wagons acting as a barrier between them and the inflammable tankers. The A34 is now on the alignment. (P.H.Swift)

96. Class 9F 2-10-0 no. 92007 is pounding up the 1 in 106 gradient with a fine clear exhaust in September 1961. It is just about to pass under the Southern Region main line, running north. (P.J.Cupper)

KINGS WORTHY

97. After years of agitation, local residents were rewarded with a station on 1st February 1909, the goods yard being completed on 29th April following. This was despite the population only rising from 438 in 1881 to 452 in 1901. Here we look southwards, one of the steep paths being evident on the right. (R.Simmonds coll.)

Kings Worthy opened February 1909	1903	1913	1923	1933
Passenger tickets issued	-	12176	8769	8294
Season tickets issued	-	*	12	-
Parcels forwarded	-	2169	2399	4766
General goods forwarded (tons)	-	597	3825	+
Coal and coke received (tons)	-	184	112	+
Other minerals received (tons)	-	2219	1748	+
General goods received (tons)	-	916	588	+
Trucks of livestock handled	-	60	20	+

+ Included with Winchester from 1932 to 1935
(* not available)

As elsewhere the loop, which here dated from 1909, was extended in 1943 but, uniquely, the old signal box was transplanted bodily.

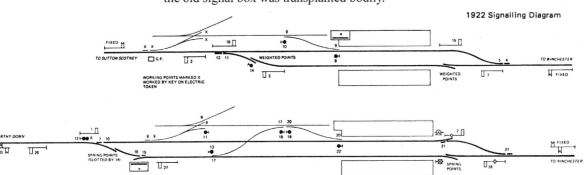

1922 Signalling Diagram

1943 Signalling Diagram

98. A northward panorama in about 1933 includes the goods yard, which had a 6-ton crane. Timber platform facings and buildings were employed owing to the embankment location. This is the position of the signal box from 1909 to 1943. (D.Thompson)

99. The box and up loop were taken out of use on 30th January 1955 and a ground frame then gave access to the yard. This is the final resting place for the box, which had been moved bodily on a trolley and then turned round. Goods traffic ceased on 1st October 1962. (T.B.Sands)

100. The building became rather delapidated towards the end of its life. The small shed was used for lamps and bicycles; it had earlier housed the ground frame shown on the left of the 1922 diagram. Pumps and hydraulic rams from a neighbouring firm were despatched frequently. (L.Elsey)

101. On the left is evidence of the dock having been extended. This had been done in 1931 when, on one occasion, 28 horse boxes formed a train from here. *City of Truro* has just left the remaining platform in 1957, the path to it being on the right. (M.Esau)

NORTH OF WINCHESTER

102. No. 2240 was a regular engine on the route and is seen drifting gently downhill through Winnall. Few would believe that this cutting had been constructed for double track.
(Hampshire Chronicle)

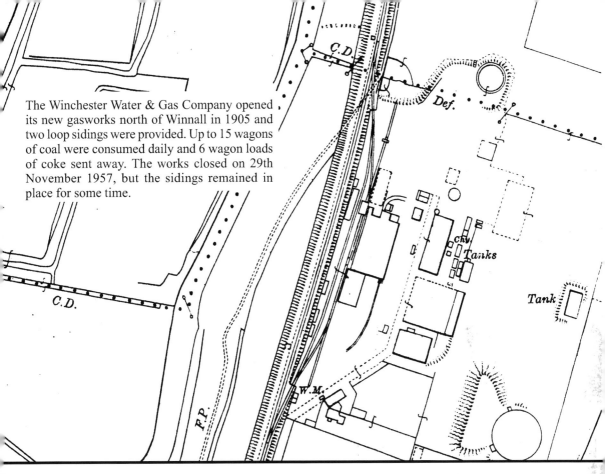

The Winchester Water & Gas Company opened its new gasworks north of Winnall in 1905 and two loop sidings were provided. Up to 15 wagons of coal were consumed daily and 6 wagon loads of coke sent away. The works closed on 29th November 1957, but the sidings remained in place for some time.

103. Shovels were the order of the day when a branch was constructed from Winnall in 1918 to serve a military camp and hospital on Morn Hill. The USA joined the War a few months before it ended - some of their troops were found a useful task. (Unknown)

104. As part of the line capacity improvements of 1943, double track was laid north from Winchester, through the tunnel and just beyond. The military line mentioned in caption 103 curved to the right near the hedge. Winnall Industrial Estate is in embryo in the background. (I.D.Beale)

105. Emerging from the north end of the 447yd long Winchester Tunnel is no. 2240, on 9th June 1947. This end of the tunnel was used by a gun club after closure. (G.L.Hoare)

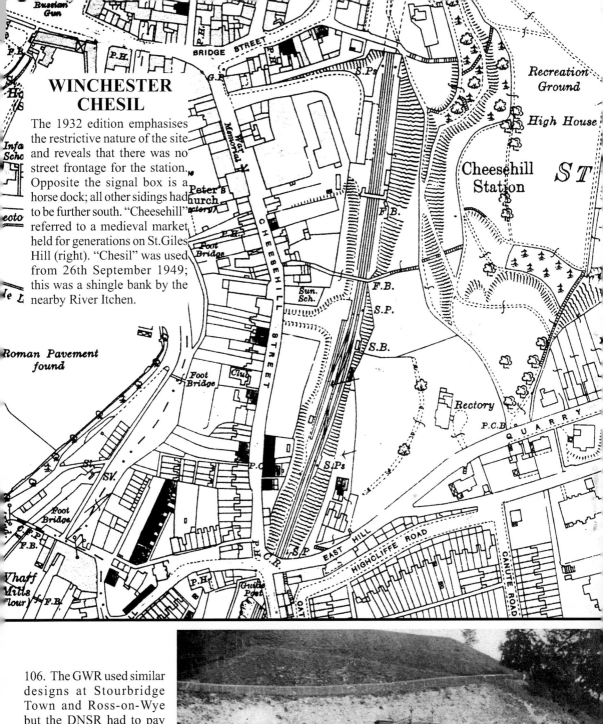

WINCHESTER CHESIL

The 1932 edition emphasises the restrictive nature of the site and reveals that there was no street frontage for the station. Opposite the signal box is a horse dock; all other sidings had to be further south. "Cheesehill" referred to a medieval market held for generations on St.Giles Hill (right). "Chesil" was used from 26th September 1949; this was a shingle bank by the nearby River Itchen.

Recreation Ground

High House

Cheesehill Station

Roman Pavement found

106. The GWR used similar designs at Stourbridge Town and Ross-on-Wye but the DNSR had to pay for this one. The station was a terminus from 1885 to 1891, when the chalk was reprofiled to accommodate a down platform safely. (Winchester Museum)

107. Until 1910, all trains changed locomotives here but many continued to do so until 1950, the engines laying over at the horse dock. Class T1 0-4-4T no. 358 may have just worked an up train and the crew would have suffered the usual long wait in the tunnel while a GWR engine was attached to the train. (N.Shepherd)

108. Seen from the public footbridge (see map) on 16th August 1948 is no. 2289 with coal probably destined for the gasworks. The single line to Shawford Junction is to the right of the brake van. (F.E.Box)

109. *City of Truro* enters the tunnel in September 1957, having passed the signal that was unusually not at the top of the post. This was for sighting reasons, as was the white background panel. The station area is now occupied by a multi-storey car park. (E.Best)

110. A 1961 photograph features the 1892 footbridge and the down side waiting room and urinal. There were no point rods or signal wires between 1923 and 1933, as the GWR tested an all-electric Siemens system in that period. The box had 16 miniature levers and an automatic route setting system in which 15 routes were programmed. (M.Hale)

111. Photographed from East Hill bridge on 27th February 1960 is no. 6313 entering the last single line section on its journey to Eastleigh. The line on the right is for goods only. (C.Haydon)

Winchester	1903	1913	1923	1933
Passenger tickets issued	28383	37110	30021	13171
Season tickets issued	*	*	63	6
Parcels forwarded	17565	23165	19962	33414
General goods forwarded (tons)	6787	6825	5979	2908
Coal and coke received (tons)	1766	9124	5478	11981
Other minerals received (tons)	18206	5497	2857	9065
General goods received (tons)	7415	13881	15483	13358
Trucks of livestock handled	171	206	146	233

(* not available)

112. The first signal box was near the urinal seen in picture 110. This is the 1923 box, which had been enlarged from two to three front windows in 1942 to accommodate a 27-lever frame in place of the 1933 22-lever one. The wooden post evident in the previous picture had been changed to steel by the time this photograph was taken in 1966. (C.Haydon)

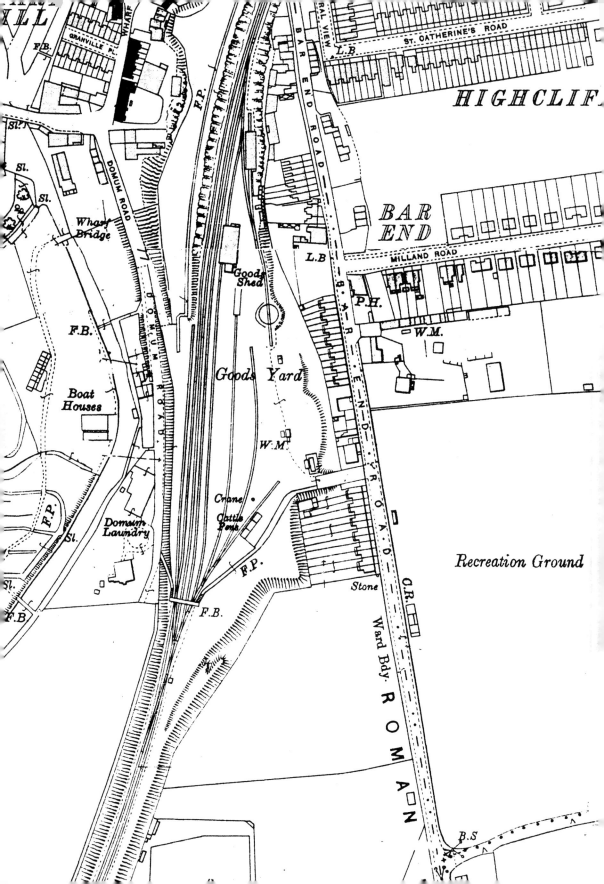

BAR END GOODS

← This map continues from the bottom of the previous one and has the passenger line on the left at the bottom. It is parallel to a long headshunt at the north of which is a ground frame which allowed trains in and out of the yard at its south end. The engine shed is north of the turntable, which was 42ft long. This was changed to a 65ft model on 29th September 1947. It was little used after 1950 and was moved to Nine Elms in about 1955.

113. Two Didcot engines were usually sub-shedded here, back to back, and one set of coaches remained overnight and on Sundays. This is the view from the public footpath on 5th October 1947; the shed was closed on 8th June 1953 and demolished in about 1955. (E.Branch)

114. A northward panorama from the public footbridge in 1948 includes the 6-ton crane. The wagons on the left are in Simmons & Gifford's siding, which is to the left of the running line. The weigh-house is on the right. As many as ten wagons loaded with beer from Burton-on-Trent arrived daily at one time. (F.E.Box)

115. A small one-ton crane was available inside the shed which was photographed in 1964. The yard was in use until 4th April 1966; making the route south thereof the last section to open and the last to close. The shed was still standing in 1998, in use by a scrap merchant. (E.Best)

116. The line ran at the foot of St. Catherine's Hill and had to be moved westwards 60ft in February 1937 to allow the Winchester Bypass to be built in its place. No. 2201 was recorded on 5th March 1960, running south on Shawford Viaduct, which stands today as a monument to the tenacity of the enterprising directors of the DNSR. It was built of concrete, with a brick facing. (D.Cross)

Other views of Shawford Junction can be found in the *Woking to Southampton* album from Middleton Press.

SHAWFORD JUNCTION

117. The original winding bypass is in the background as class 4 no. 76010 works empty wagons from Winchester to Eastleigh on 21st March 1963. The train is signalled for the relief line that was added east of the main line in 1943. The M3 now passes over this area. (C.Haydon)

118. An up train passes behind the LSWR signal box on 13th February 1954, as it enters the single line to Winchester Chesil. The GWR tried a diesel railcar on the route in 1947 but the gradients proved too severe for it. However, DMUs were used north of Newbury in the final years. (T.B.Sands)

119. Owing to congestion on the main line, DEMUs terminated at Chesil instead of City station on Saturdays in the Summer timetables of 1960 and 1961, although the station was officially closed. Departures for Southampton Terminus in 1961 were at 10.0am, 1.58 and 2.52pm. (L.Elsey)

120. As class 5 no. 73110 *The Red Knight* passes with a Waterloo to Southampton Docks boat train on 27th July 1966, we have the opportunity to examine the junction. The two lines to the Chesil route were lifted, the relief line (foreground) was connected to the down main, and then all three lines were electrified to Eastleigh and beyond. (E.Wilmshurst)

MP Middleton Press

EVOLVING THE ULTIMATE RAIL ENCYCLOPEDIA

Easebourne Lane, Midhurst, West Sussex. GU29 9AZ Tel:01730 813169

www.middletonpress.co.uk   email:info@middletonpress.co.uk
A-978 0 906520 B-978 1 873793 C-978 1 901706 D-978 1 904474 E-978 1 906008

All titles listed below were in print at time of publication - please check current availability by looking at our website - *www.middletonpress.co.uk* or by requesting a Brochure which includes our *LATEST* RAILWAY TITLES also our TRAMWAY, TROLLEYBUS, MILITARY and WATERWAYS series